PROFIT FROM PROCUREMENT

PROFIT FROM PROCUREMENT

Add 30% to Your Bottom Line by Breaking Down Silos

Alex Klein
Simon Whatson
Jose Oliveira

WILEY

For general information on our other products and services or for technical support, please contact our Customer Care Department within the United States at (800) 762-2974, outside the United States at (317) 572-3993 or fax (317) 572-4002.

Wiley publishes in a variety of print and electronic formats and by print-on-demand. Some material included with standard print versions of this book may not be included in e-books or in print-on-demand. If this book refers to media such as a CD or DVD that is not included in the version you purchased, you may download this material at http://booksupport.wiley.com. For more information about Wiley products, visit www.wiley.com.

Library of Congress Cataloging-in-Publication Data:

Names: Klein, Alex (Author of Profit from procurement), author. | Whatson, Simon, author. | Oliveira, Jose, author.
Title: Profit from procurement : add 30% to your bottom line by breaking down silos / Alex Klein, Simon Whatson, Jose Oliveira.
Description: Hoboken, New Jersey : Wiley, 2021. | Includes index.
Identifiers: LCCN 2021000246 (print) | LCCN 2021000247 (ebook) | ISBN 9781119784739 (hardback) | ISBN 9781119784982 (adobe pdf) | ISBN 9781119784913 (epub)
Subjects: LCSH: Industrial procurement. | Business logistics.
Classification: LCC HD39.5 .K534 2021 (print) | LCC HD39.5 (ebook) | DDC 658.7/2—dc23
LC record available at https://lccn.loc.gov/2021000246
LC ebook record available at https://lccn.loc.gov/2021000247

Cover design: Wiley

Printed in Great Britain by Bell and Bain Ltd, Glasgow

This book is dedicated to our wives,
Michelle, Sonja, and Inês

Contents

1

INTRODUCTION: Why Procurement, and Why Now?

What Follows Is a True Story

Many years ago, I was at a cocktail party hosted for expats in London, with my wife. Many of those present were from the big New York investment banks. At one point, I started chatting with one of these individuals.

"So, what do you do?" he asked.
"I'm a consultant." I replied.
"Consulting in which field?" he asked.

"Procurement" I replied, at which point he looked at me with an expression of disgust and said, "Excuse me while my eyes glaze over," then turned around to signal that the conversation was over.

Now, that's very rude behaviour, but that's not the point. The point is that Procurement has such a poor image that it's not even deemed worthy of a conversation by those who consider themselves to be at the top of the business food chain. Procurement is just not exciting, and it's certainly not sexy.

Well, how exciting does it have to be? How about having the potential of increasing your EBITDA by a third? How about having the resilience to keep your supply chain up and running during a global pandemic? Procurement is an enormous profitability lever, and it should be a core competence—especially in modern times, in which companies accomplish more and more through outsourced relationships.

Yet in the majority of companies, Procurement is far from optimized, and there is a massive prize to be had if we could only do a better job. Since Procurement represents between 50 and 80% of a company's costs depending on the industry, and since most savings extracted from that spend flow straight to the bottom line, then I'd say that makes it interesting!

In this chapter, we will set the scene for the book, by examining why there is an opportunity in Procurement, what the size of the prize could look like, and why many companies have failed to cash in on the promise to date. At the end of the chapter, we provide some background to the book, along with an overview of what you can expect from the remaining chapters.

Let's now step right back and examine why there is an opportunity associated with Procurement. There are, in essence, two reasons: (i) Procurement is typically a company's largest cost bucket, and (ii) in most companies, that cost bucket is not optimized. Let's look at each in turn.

Procurement Is a Company's Number One Cost, Making It a Huge Profit Lever

Procurement represents between 50 and 80% of a company's total costs, depending on the industry. That feels like a big number, but that's just because external spend is not usually counted in one place. A company's external spend contains so many things (from office supplies to raw materials to factory maintenance services to energy, fleet, marketing, and IT), fragmented across so many business units, geographies and budget lines, that it's rarely seen in aggregate **(see Figure 1.1)**.

OK, so the spend is big, but how big is the opportunity? In many companies that have not yet optimized Procurement, it can be very significant. Figure 1.1 looks at a typical manufacturing company, with revenues indexed to 100. Well, if you simply subtract from that 100 your EBIT (or add back in your losses), then take out

Procurement Spend as a % of Total Cash Outflows

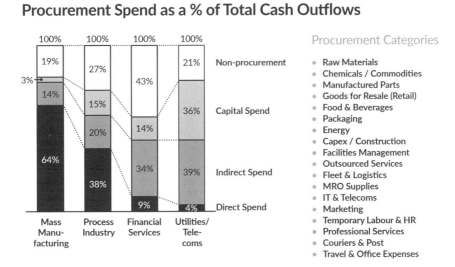

Source: *Efficio client experience*

Figure 1.1   Procurement Spend as a Percentage of Total Cash Outflows

depreciation and your whole salaries and wages bill, then what's left of the 100 is by definition externally procured. In this example (**see Figure 1.2**), that amounts to 60 … 60% of the revenue!

The next question is, how much can you take out of that 60? Well, a common mistake is to assume that "10% should be possible." Maybe 10% is possible, but not on the whole 60 of spend, at least not in the medium term, because some spends will be non-addressable or locked in, and there is always a "tail" of specialist one-off suppliers. These non-addressable spends can be significant, so it's safe to assume that maybe 60% of the 60 is addressable in the medium term. If your organization is global, you may also have a collection of very small, remote geographies whose spend may be too small to merit addressing in the medium term, which could reduce the 60% further.

In terms of how much can be saved, this of course varies by category and by company. But, long story short, a company that has not optimized Procurement, can look to take roughly 10% out of its addressable spend. In the worked example in Figure 1.2, that equates to a saving of 3.6 from an addressable spend of 36 (60% of 60). Given that the

Procurement's EBIT Impact
Procurement Spend, Savings Potential, and EBIT Impact
(Indexed Manufacturing Example)

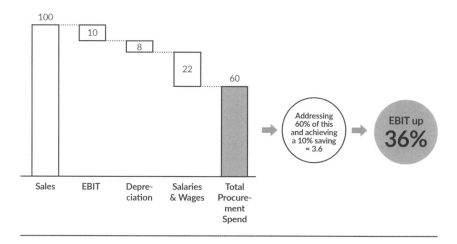

Figure 1.2   Procurement's EBIT Impact

company had an EBIT of 10 going in, then that's a 36% uplift on a 10% margin. And that's before you factor in any Capex savings (which of course hit EBIT only indirectly).

The beauty of Procurement is that this opportunity (or your spend) is spread across some 40 or so spend categories. This comprises a very diverse set of things (from Office Supplies to Logistics Providers to Raw Materials to Components …), each with totally different suppliers and its own internal stakeholders. Since a Procurement effort is best structured around category teams (see Chapter 3: Sourcing Execution), then this creates a natural portfolio effect across your target—one category may fail, but another will over-deliver. This portfolio effect is critical in Procurement economics, in that it significantly mitigates the risk of non-delivery.

At the end of the day, it would be difficult to find opportunities with as much potential impact on EBITDA as Procurement, without the need to reduce headcount, close offices, or make major investments. So, at least on paper, the Procurement opportunity is significant.

That's all very well in theory. But what about in practice? How do I know that the 10% is actually *there*? *Why* is there an opportunity in this cost base? Answer: Because in many companies, Procurement is not optimized. Let's examine why that is the case.

Why Is Procurement Not Optimized?

The opportunity in Procurement exists because in many companies, Procurement is not optimized. There are a number of reasons for this:

- Procurement comes from an administrative background, and often lacks the remit to take a strategic or proactive approach.
- Procurement therefore doesn't have the right cross-functional operating model, and sometimes adopts unhelpful mindsets.
- This results in an under-investment in people and tools, creating a vicious cycle of under-performance and under-investment.
- The end result is a spend base that's not optimized—not aggregated across locations, and with inconsistent specifications and dated supplier relationships.

Let's explore some of these points in a little more detail.

Remit

The point regarding remit is fundamental: it asks the question, what is *expected* of Procurement? Unfortunately, many Procurement functions do *not* have a remit to "work with the budget holders to proactively optimize their cost base using the full suite of supply and demand levers." Rather, the expectation is that Procurement will come in at the last minute to negotiate and execute the contract. That remit will allow Procurement to achieve maybe 25% of its potential. And therein lies the problem, or the opportunity ... the Procurement function is probably doing a good job—but based on an overly narrow remit.

The root of this problem is that Procurement's history lies in administration. The function started life as a mechanism to legally procure goods and services on behalf of the business and is therefore seen as a support function—one that ensures that supplier contracts get signed and materials show up. Over time, Procurement teams have been built on these administrative foundations as their functions have evolved. In many organizations, the budget holder actually makes most of the decisions—from deciding what part is needed, to deciding to go with the OEM (Original Equipment Manufacturer) part to, very often, talking to the OEM and agreeing to a price. Only then is Procurement brought in, to close the deal, sign the contract, and order the part. And that's the typical remit … which ensures that probably 80% of the cost is already locked in by the time Procurement comes to the table, thereby severely constraining Procurement's potential contribution from the get-go.

Given this restrictive remit, it comes as no surprise then, that Procurement often hasn't developed anywhere near the right cross-functional operating model: see Chapter 5: Operating Model, for a more detailed discussion of this. To make matters worse, in the absence of a clear role, buyers can sometimes adopt unhelpful mindsets. Instead of adopting a service mentality along the lines of "I am here to help you with your spend," there is often a mindset based on perceived authority.

Mindset

We've seen unhelpful Procurement mindsets at countless companies; the most common ones I would describe as "the policeman" and the "Procurement professional."

The policeman is a historical legacy. Most Procurement organizations were set up to help get control of external spend, with a focus on purchase orders and necessary draconian policies of "if it doesn't go through Procurement, it doesn't go through." This has set them up for decades-long fights with stakeholders; fights in which Procurement is the policeman, chasing down the non-compliant stakeholders (sounds like a Procurement Blade Runner!).

As a result, many Procurement teams have cast themselves (often unintentionally) in a "policeman" capacity vis-à-vis "the spenders." Nowadays, this legacy mindset really doesn't wash with sophisticated and intelligent stakeholders in functions such as Engineering, Manufacturing, Technology, or Marketing. In fact, the opposite is required—a collaborative, open, intelligent approach, not a "you have to go through Procurement" approach. To this day, I see vestiges of this mindset in Procurement teams, and it's not helping the cause.

The other thing that doesn't help is when Procurement positions itself as too much of a profession. Rather than credentializing Procurement, this can sometimes create a barrier—the message here being, "We have techniques that you guys don't understand" and "We're better negotiators than you are." I've found that the strongest Procurement people are the ones who never feel the need to mention their professional skills. They just relate well to the stakeholder, and they do good work.

These somewhat dysfunctional mindsets, when coupled with an already weak remit, can act to severely undermine Procurement's potential impact.

Vicious Cycle ... and Opportunity

The lack of remit, the lack of cross-functional engagement, and, ultimately, the lack of impact of Procurement, have in turn led to a vicious cycle of under-investment in the function. In many organizations, Procurement is therefore seen as a strictly back office function that's largely ignored by senior management.

But what this historical neglect brings with it is an enormous opportunity. Most of the external spend will be ripe for Strategic Sourcing: the spend will not have been leveraged or aggregated across countries or manufacturing plants. The specifications will be outdated, "what Engineering has always used;" and there will be longstanding supplier relationships that are never tendered, ready to be shaken up with a bit of competition. In short, significant savings potential will exist across the entire third party spend.

But of course, to capture that potential, you need to work backwards and fix the remit, fix the resources available to Procurement, and fix the investment level in Procurement. We need to find a better way. Well, the good news is, that better way has been around for over 30 years.

The Birth of Strategic Sourcing—Dawn of a New Era ... or Not?

Back in the 1980s, a new way emerged for Procurement when General Motors placed its engineers and buyers in cross-functional teams and told them to "go to town" on components, changing the specifications, changing the drawings, bidding GM's combined demands in the market globally—and it worked magically and gave birth to "Global Sourcing." This was soon replaced by "Strategic Sourcing," but the concept was the same—work cross-functionally to problem-solve a chunk of the cost away, please. It's now the bread-and-butter of the auto OEMs and their direct suppliers.

This model is still widely held up as Procurement best practice today. But, outside of Big Auto, the large pharma companies, and select multi-national manufacturing companies, few have reached a truly "world class" level of sophistication in Procurement—neither in direct spend nor in the "indirects" arena. We all know what best practice looks like, because companies like GM and Ford have been doing it for half a century. At Ford Motor Company, the CPO sits on the board. Procurement is seen as career-enhancing, and the Procurement function has strong people who are able to execute cross-functionally. The savings even seem to be traceable to the P&L! And yet, it seems, most of us aren't able to replicate this success. Why is that?

One reason is simply that Ford and GM have no choice; they have to be good at Procurement. The Big Auto OEMs buy and assemble a huge volume of parts from around the globe, and they've been operating in an environment with very tight margins (with long periods of losses) for decades. That's why they're truly committed to Procurement from the top down, there is very strong Procurement leadership, there are high-caliber resources who rotate in and out of the function, the function is career-enhancing, working cross-functionally is in its DNA, and execution is of a high quality. All driven by economic necessity, which in many sectors, particularly growth-based and technology sectors, doesn't exist to the same degree.

A second reason why so many companies have failed to reach best practice is that they genuinely tried but failed to do it properly or fully. Some didn't get the right level of sponsorship or investment into the function that was required. Others yet, and there are many, have declared victory when they haven't earned it, which then blocks further progression in those companies.

Bad Best Practice

There is often a perception, particularly among $1 billion plus revenue companies, that their Procurement is "already best in class," Strategic Sourcing has been done, and "we have it all under control." There is a tendency for Procurement to say, "We've done a lot already, there's not much left here, we're close to best practice." Personally, I've probably had more than 100 Procurement leaders tell me this directly, and it's a problem, because they get away with it! The C-Suite views Procurement as a technical discipline and has "full trust that our CPO is taking care of it." In reality, that's just what the CPO communicates upwards, and it's taken as gospel because he/she is a Procurement professional, and presumably they know what they're doing.

My personal belief is that this phenomenon—call it defensiveness or what you may—blocks many billions of dollars of value being delivered through Procurement globally. I call it "bad best practice," and it's surprisingly common. It's when Procurement functions falsely believe that they've "already adopted best practice." The most common area where this plays out is in Strategic Sourcing. I have personally met scores of Procurement leaders who have been given the "Seven-Step Sourcing Methodology" by one of the big consulting firms. These approaches make a lot of sense (and they're all pretty much identical, by the way), but they have to be applied properly. Handing out cookbooks does not make good cooks.

There are other, often very large organizations, including by the 1990s some of the larger auto OEMs, in which the sourcing process has become just a process—very institutionalized, but reduced to a box-ticking exercise. I've seen examples of the work of sourcing teams in organizations that religiously but mindlessly apply a rigorous sourcing process. They have a baseline, they have a supply market study, they've created a stakeholder map, and they have a sourcing strategy. But the baseline is incomplete and it's unclear what the total spend is, the supply market study is interesting but in no way informs the sourcing strategy, the stakeholder map has sat in a file for three months never to be re-looked at, and the sourcing strategy is to bundle the volume and beat up the suppliers.

Bad best practice is a terrible thing, because it blocks *real* best practice from being put in place. And it's a remarkably common phenomenon. Many times, companies truly believe they have done all the right things. In other instances, CPOs dress up their achievements as a defense mechanism against external consultants or other perceived threats. In all cases it acts as a value blockage.

So, where do we go from here? We've stated that there may be a large opportunity, we've explained how this opportunity has come about, and we've shown that there is a commonly accepted definition of Procurement best practice, but few have managed to attain this gold standard.

The rest of this book looks forward to answering the questions, "How do we get from here to there?," "How do we maximize the profit potential of Procurement?," and "What are the fundamental building blocks we need to have in place in order to succeed?"

Why Now?

But you may ask, what's new in all this? Procurement? That's been around for decades. Why this book, and why now?

The answer to this question is that, while this book was written during the global COVID-19 pandemic, its content and messages go well beyond this and are just the accumulated "wisdom" of three Procurement professionals. On the other hand, COVID-19 has clearly put a spotlight on Procurement. As we watched supply chains grind to a halt across the globe, it was easy to spot those who were prepared, those who had their supply chains in order … and the many others who were not prepared, and who were blind-sided by the crisis.

From a Procurement perspective, COVID-19 puts into partial question some of the core supply chain concepts companies have worked hard to implement over the last four decades: JIT (just-in-time) delivery, single sourcing, "best cost country sourcing" from geographically far-flung locations … these concepts drive cost out of the supply chain, but at the expense of increasing exposure to risk. A global disruption like COVID-19 is likely to then test those tightly strung supply chains to the limit.

What the pandemic showed again is that Procurement sits at the heart of the company, it's the interface between the company and its suppliers and service providers—and as companies outsource more and more, the number and scale of service providers grows. Now, the COVID-19 pandemic has made us ask questions like "Do we have enough control over all our key supplier relationships and contracts?," "Do we have contingency suppliers who can rapidly ramp up capacity for us?" and "Do we have a strong Logistics partner?"

It's commonly accepted now that there will be more global pandemics to come, so let's be sure to learn our lessons from the current one. But also, why not use the post-COVID-19 era to revisit our Procurement cost base? Now is a time for everyone to look at their costs, so why not combine it with a review of our supply chain resilience in the face of a global crisis.

So now *does* seem like a good time to revisit Procurement, and maybe ask "How far have we really come?" How big is the opportunity, where does it lie, and how do we capture it? These are the questions this book seeks to answer.

But while the pandemic partly provided the impetus for writing this book, at the end of the day, none of the messages in this book are "COVID-specific." The pandemic has shone a light on Procurement, but what it has revealed was already there. This is not a "COVID-era book," and we will not be discussing the pandemic further.

About This Book

This book is not an academic book. It represents the distilled opinions of three Procurement consultants who between them have many decades of direct and highly relevant experience. But the views and ideas expressed in this book are not facts. Indeed, you may work for a world-class company to whom many of the statements don't apply. This book is about typical situations, based on what we've found throughout our combined careers, and it's squarely aimed at the "bottom 80%," rather than the top 20%.

The central thesis of this book is that Procurement is a major underexploited profit lever and in order to maximize its potential, a number of components must be in place, including a fit-for-purpose Procurement function that executes cross-functionally and delivers credible benefits to the business. From there, the book explores each of these components and how to make them work in practice.

The book is aimed at the entire C-Suite and is relevant not only to the CPO, but to the CFO, CEO, COO, and CIO. Why? Because (i) they all stand to gain significantly, and (ii) the CPO needs the rest of the C-Suite if he/she is to succeed. The book is also aimed at the Private Equity Operating Partner (or any other professional) looking to leverage Procurement for EBITDA improvements. We have therefore written the book in an executive style—not from a Procurement perspective, but from a cross-functional perspective. We hope that the book speaks to the entire C-Suite and helps to further educate CEOs and CFOs, in particular, about the opportunity inherent in Procurement.

This book is not an all-encompassing guide to all matters "Procurement." Look at it as a collection of essays on key topics. All of these topics are of relevance to the CPO. The CFO and other executives might prefer to dip in and out of specific chapters, but we would argue that the Introduction and Conclusion, and the chapters on People, Sourcing Execution, Operating Model, Savings Realization, and Cross-Functional Change are highly relevant to all.

We have tried to pepper the book with relevant and interesting client anecdotes, without boring you with too much detail. Finally, the three authors are management consultants. We think this gives us a very good perspective, since we've seen all the issues discussed here with multiple clients many times over. It also means that we have a large toolbox of consulting frameworks. What we've found is that a small number of these frameworks have proven particularly powerful in transforming Procurement. So, at certain points in the book we intend to share with the reader the "secrets" of some of the more successful Procurement consulting frameworks, and how to get use from them in practice.

We're keen in this book to move beyond the hype, so our intent has been very much to be honest about the Procurement opportunity and how to capture it, and to keep the advice pragmatic and useful. Our aim was to "tell it like it is, warts and all," the "No b-s!," C-level guide to Procurement. We hope we've fulfilled that aim. We'd love to hear from you, but please don't write to tell us the following:

- **"You're such a bunch of consultants"**—We know that, we can't help it! We don't think we know all the answers, but we think we have a valid external perspective; we have humbly showcased only a small number of consulting frameworks that have proved effective over the years.
- **"You're repetitive"**—Yes, and that's a good thing! There are certain themes that run through the entire book, revisited in Chapter 14: Conclusion, that are touched on in multiple chapters ... and these are the things we'd like you to remember; hence the repetition.
- **"The book isn't exhaustive"**—No, it isn't. This is not a structured textbook. View it more as a collection of essays on some of the most important topics to take into account when transforming Procurement.
- **"My company is very good at Procurement. We've already done much of what you're advocating"**—Great. We recognize that many companies have sophisticated Procurement functions; this book is aimed at those that don't and are looking to maximize Procurement's potential, as well as those who do but want to get some insight into what other companies are doing that they might learn from.
- **"You're down on Procurement"**—No, we're not. We're down on bad Procurement, and Procurement whose potential is not maximized, and sometimes we're quite vocal about that. But we are champions of Procurement teams that have devoted their careers to the cause.
- **"All your examples feature simple indirect spend categories"**—This is true. We tried to feature more complex direct materials case studies, but they're not universally understood and require more explanation, which makes it awkward to refer to them. Hence, we've relied more on indirect category examples, such as Travel, MRO, and Office Supplies. While not "strategic," these categories are in fact quite complex and served us well in illustrating our points.

■ **"You're too focused on savings"**—The premise of this book is that Procurement is a significant and underexploited profit lever, which does put savings center-stage. Of course, Procurement has other objectives, as discussed in Chapter 8: Non-savings Priorities. But we firmly believe that it's the bottom-line contribution to profitability that puts Procurement on the map, and that is the central thesis of this book.

Of course, you can write to us anyway, but hopefully the above helps to clarify where we're coming from, and what this book is and isn't trying to be.

****

In the following pages, this book will examine the Procurement Transformation journey from all angles and asks the questions that the C-level executive should be asking:

■ Where is the opportunity, and how big is it?
■ How do I capture this opportunity and its cost savings in practice?
■ Why do so many companies get it wrong, and how do I get it right?
■ How do I build the right team in Procurement, and how do I work effectively cross-functionally?
■ How do I ensure the savings actually flow to the bottom line?
■ What Procurement technologies do we and don't we need?
■ How do we use Procurement to minimize supply chain risk and drive non-savings agendas like Sustainability?
■ What can we learn from Private Equity and its approach to Procurement?

The central theme that runs right through this book is cross-functionality. Procurement's potential cannot be maximized while operating within a functional silo. That means that the entire C-Suite needs to engage with Procurement, and vice versa. Which is why this is not a book for just the CPO... Procurement is an inherently cross-functional endeavor, and success is only possible if the C-Suite works together.

We hope you enjoy the rest of the book.

2

AMBITION: Ensuring You Are Set Up for Success

A Dirty Procurement Word

I attended a Procurement panel event last year where the audience was putting questions to half a dozen senior and well-respected people from the Procurement profession. The audience was itself full of successful Procurement people, and it's one of those evenings where you learn a lot about the profession.

The theme of the evening was the future of Procurement and what people should be considering when deciding on the next priorities for their function. In other words, **What should Procurement's ambition be?**

Most of the panel were CPOs from large companies—a couple of the brands were household names. The panel had been generally agreeable up until that point, but thankfully it contained a couple of characters who are known to hold strong views and not to be shy about voicing them.

One question and answer round I found particularly fascinating was when the following question was asked: **"Do you think that Procurement should be measured on savings?"**

Now, the first reason I thought this was interesting was because of the way the question was asked. The questioner might as well have added the words "surely not!" at the end, such was the tone used. It's funny because savings (or any other word to denote monetary benefits) has become a bit of a dirty word in Procurement in recent years, as if people in the profession are ashamed to talk about it.

It's certainly less fashionable to talk about savings at events such as these, where surely there must be some new and exciting things for Procurement to aspire to after all these years!

Perhaps that is because sometimes savings programs have failed, or CPOs have been unable to translate savings into wider business-speak and therefore constantly come up against internal brick walls. Then there are the CFOs who have "learned never to trust a Procurement savings number." So, all of a sudden, we have an entire industry nervous to associate themselves with the thing they all thought they specifically existed for just a few years ago. It's an interesting phenomenon, and I was eager to see how the debate would play out.

First up was the successful CPO of one of the world's largest engineering services company. She immediately declared that her function was "past that." Indeed, apparently her latest Procurement strategy didn't even have a savings number in it. She went on to explain that the success metrics they use are engagement level with the business, automation, and quality. Finally, and only as she was offering some closing thoughts, did she admit that savings were sometimes used as a metric, but only "where appropriate" and for certain projects.

The microphone was then passed to the CPO of a water utility to answer the same question. He seemed to be just as keen not to be seen as a savings CPO. I think we are "way past that," he said. Apparently, his function gets measured on many other elements such as customer satisfaction, supply chain satisfaction, sustainability, and even carbon neutrality. But then he too began to introduce a bit of nuance towards the end of his answer.

"I think many CEOs and CFOs see savings as a given," he said. "You have to be, and remain, cost competitive in the market," he explained, before adding, "I think other types of value are secondary to that, in reality." With that final comment his voice trailed off, and he appeared to brace himself for reaction from the audience and his fellow panelists. After all, he had just done a bit of a U-turn and sort of admitted to a hundred of his peers that savings were in fact the number one priority of his function!

The third speaker nailed it, for me. He was the CPO of one of the large supermarket chains in the UK; he spoke confidently. "The fact is, savings are important," he explained. "If you inherit a Procurement team that doesn't have a standing in the business then your ability to get credibility rests on setting a three-year value for money improvement, call it savings if you like, and achieving it." He said that once you deliver that, you then get permission to expand into things such as driving innovation in the supply chain, having goals around supplier satisfaction and all the other worthy goals a Procurement team should aspire to as well. He then talked some more, but was simply re-emphasizing his central point that the only way to get credibility in the organization first as a CPO is to drive cost improvements.

Yes, there are other things that the Procurement function can and should eventually do to add value in ways beyond savings, but they come second.

Walk, Then Run

What I learned from that exchange confirmed to me what I have seen throughout my career as a Procurement consultant. Namely, many CPOs and Procurement professionals aspire to be something other than people who save money. That is excellent, because there is certainly more to Procurement than saving money, but much care is needed.

The people on this panel were successful CPOs with mature Procurement functions, and each of them had established themselves in their respective businesses and earned the right to go beyond savings in pursuit of more corporate value. However, in public these days, even these people throw in the savings piece as a bit of an afterthought, as if it isn't important, like the first two speakers on the panel. And this is the wrong message.

This is a peculiar state of affairs. After all, didn't Procurement initially exist to be the commercial conscience of its organization? The answer to that is: yes, it did. When companies realized just how much of their spend was going to third parties, they saw an opportunity to professionalize the way they purchase—to generate synergies and to remove cost.

As we saw in the previous chapter, it was the auto companies that were first to the party but almost every other industry since has set up Procurement functions to help their organizations spend money better and more efficiently. As some Procurement functions became more advanced, they earned the right to expand their remit and justifiably so.

But we have seen many examples of CPOs trying to skip the step of establishing themselves as effective savings CPOs, going straight to attempting to claim ownership of all sorts of different areas that have little to do with savings. If your CPO has a vision for his or her department, how much of it were you expecting to be in there? The chances are if there are any surprises, your CPO is probably trying to run before they can walk.

CPOs need to be realistic about their starting point and the need to walk first, exactly as the supermarket CPO on our panel said. Being recognized and respected as the commercial conscience of the organization is paramount; it's the main event. And why wouldn't it be?

As we explain in this book, and indeed the very first chapter, Procurement can boost profits by a whopping 30%, or more in an organization where it's done really well. This is why the Procurement function exists first and foremost and, unless a Procurement function is already achieving that 30% boost, it needs to retain that as the single biggest priority in the ambition.

It's worth clarifying at this point what we mean by savings. Put simply, it is ensuring the company is getting better value from the supply market. It is not restricted to price reduction, though that certainly is a saving. It can (and must) also include savings on total cost—for example, you buy a more expensive part that lasts longer, thus costing less over the life-time of a product that costs less but doesn't last as long—and even cashflow improvements, if cash is important to the company. We go into more detail on savings and how to track them in Chapter 9: Savings Realization.

The difficulty of understanding your starting point is compounded by the fact that Procurement functions can sometimes think they are better than they really are. And this is not because they are arrogant in general, it's because they have a different understanding of what Procurement is achieving in their company today than most of their peers in other functions.

For example, Procurement often quotes savings figures it has delivered when asked about achievements, but how much of these savings are believed by the rest of the company? That is critical. Without that common understanding, the savings will not give you credibility. And if a Procurement function aspires to pursue other causes than savings, it needs to be credible on savings first.

But it's not all Procurement's fault. If Procurement tends to overvalue itself, then companies also tend to undervalue Procurement. But, unfortunately, it's up to Procurement to redress that balance.

In fact, to truly understand the starting point, it's necessary to know what value the business currently ascribes to Procurement.

What are they expecting Procurement to deliver?

What Procurement ultimately wants to deliver doesn't really matter until it can firstly deliver what the business wants, and that is usually a commercial benefit to the business. So, one of the most crucial things a CPO can do when setting the ambition is aligning that starting point with peers and stakeholders.

As our supermarket CPO said, delivering from that starting point gives you the credibility to expand your mandate and remit and go further than just savings.

What to Aim For

Given that the level of ambition is dependent on your starting point, it's useful at this point to examine some different starting points that are real life examples. Of course, the ambition will depend on other aspects too—such as corporate direction, size, and quality of team—but the starting point is often just a function of these. These examples will provide good indicators of what your ambition should be.

Firstly, we will look at a Procurement function with lots of history, a sizeable team, but no real standing in the business. Next, a Procurement function that has started to gain traction with its organization through two years of impressive cost savings delivery in a company that traditionally had no professional Procurement, and finally a Procurement organization that has consistently delivered year-on-year commercial benefits for its company for a decade.

The function with no standing

Someone I know joined as a CPO for a large global pharmaceutical company a few years ago, reporting to the CFO. Procurement was already a recognized function in the company. It had a fairly good-sized team for the spend, it had a good mix of strategic and operational resources both centrally and in the regions, and individuals within the function had good relationships with some of their counterparts in the business.

Prior to the new CPO's arrival, the Procurement function was reporting impressive savings—in fact upwards of 10% on some categories. They also had well-documented Procurement policies and procedures. The CPO had achieved some stellar results at previous blue-chip companies, leading Procurement to new heights in those organizations. On the surface, all the ingredients were there for this new CPO to aim to take Procurement to "the next level" straight away: that is to say, beyond savings. But this particular CPO didn't make that mistake. Rather, he was realistic about his starting point.

The reality was that Procurement was not involved in any of the important business discussions because it was not fully trusted. Key decisions around which drugs to bring to market, commercial viability of those drugs, which suppliers to invest in, and managing supply chain risk were not yet within their remit. Crucially, the savings they achieved were either not believed or not visible to the people in the business who mattered. The CPO knew this, and knew it before he had taken on the job. So, his first priority was to make the Procurement function known for simply delivering a cost benefit. From there he would build credibility.

Within the first two years, as well as cleaning up some of the administrative processes and reinvigorating his team and how it interacts with the business, he had delivered a program of savings that most of the company was behind and could see the benefits of. From there, the remit and mandate had expanded organically, as peers had seen how the approach that had helped to deliver cost benefit could also be used to help better manage supply chain risk with key suppliers—something that has a direct impact on revenue.

This is an example of a CPO who was confident and humble enough to understand the starting point of Procurement in his business and set the correct priorities and ambition. Had he tried to impose his function on other areas immediately, I'm certain his function would not be delivering as much value as it is today.

The function with traction

A FinTech company founded two decades earlier had never professionalized its Procurement until two years ago, when they hired some consultants to strategically address their largest buckets of spend. The one-year program was a big success and, as a follow-on, the company decided to build capability inhouse by hiring a permanent CPO and a team around her. After one year, that Procurement team has made a valuable and recognizable contribution to de-risking the business plan, which had been put at risk due to a drop in revenues in a major business unit due to consumer trends.

In the early days of the first program, almost no one in the company had confidence that Procurement could deliver anything, but by now the value Procurement could bring in professionalizing supplier relationships and driving cost out was becoming clear to all.

I spoke to the CPO recently, after a year in the role, and she was pretty clear on where she wanted to go. She told me that, ultimately, she sees Procurement's biggest contribution as being in product development. With products that are driven almost entirely by technological advancements that happen very quickly in a market full of start-ups with very low barriers to entry, she believes Procurement is ideally placed to be the ones on top of where the next innovation is coming from and which suppliers to invest in.

Product managers in different functions do this role today but there is so much Procurement can contribute to this, she thinks. But while Procurement has driven significant cost benefits for a couple of years, there is more to be done on that front, and the business expects it. That is why, for the next year at least, cost remains her number one priority, albeit from a different angle. Her view is that a lot of the pre-contracting processes around spend visibility, contract renewals, sourcing process, and pipeline development are working well and are embedded in the organization to the extent that they will continue to deliver cost benefit with less attention from her team. She believes the biggest cost benefits to be had now are post-contract supplier management. And this is where the immediate focus of her team will be.

Cleverly, she also thinks that by proving her team's credentials in this area—gaining trust for managing some of the company's most critical supplier relationships—she will find it easier to position her function to support the product teams later and their work identifying the next innovation in the market. It's worth noting that this area would itself have been out of bounds just two years prior.

Procurement has earned the right to set up and join performance reviews with business-critical suppliers at this company through the analytics, change management, and commercial skills it has shown in the pre-contracting space.

So again, we have a CPO with a refreshingly realistic view of her starting point, who eventually will move the Procurement function further up the value chain to add yet more value to the business. Her priority now is continuing to earn the credibility to do that.

The mature function

There is one company I've had the pleasure of working with that has created a well-oiled Strategic Sourcing engine at the core of its function that has been the guardian of cost competitiveness for the organization for almost a decade. If you speak to the CPO, there is more to be done, but he knows how the Procurement function is perceived—a competent, if occasionally over-zealous function that has contributed significant and unprecedented commercial firepower to the organization.

The CPO is an influencer at board level and has the ear of the CFO. So, what now for this Procurement function?

It goes without saying that keeping on top of cost is a key priority, but arguably they are much further on than the Fintech company in the previous example. That means that the machine can run itself with just a little fine-tuning here and there. People in the wider organization are looking to and indeed expecting Procurement to raise its game yet again, such is the success of the function so far.

So, what is the ambition of this function? Well, they are numerous, but they definitely include maintaining cost competitiveness. The second is refining their demand forecasting tool to further reduce maintenance costs across the business and even start to generate revenue.

By analyzing and modeling data as to where failures are likely to occur, the Procurement function has worked closely with the supply chain and the maintenance function to make it many times more efficient. This is a sophisticated tool and methodology the CPO has the ambition to sell to other companies in the industry and generate revenue.

The company, being publicly regulated, is also under pressure to demonstrate its credentials in sustainability. Again, Procurement has ambitions and permission to take the lead here and has begun to weave sustainability requirements into the sourcing and supplier performance management processes which it then reports on. This in turn strengthens the hand of the company in its periodic negotiations with the regulator.

These sorts of value contributions from Procurement are hugely significant, and it's because of the trust and credibility Procurement has built up over many years that it has had the ability to have this type of ambition and deliver these results.

Getting Buy-In

If setting the right ambition is important, then getting buy-in to that ambition from others is arguably even more so. That is because, as we say throughout this book, Procurement—almost more than any other department—must work cross-functionally in any organization to be successful. If you take the simple ambition of cost reduction, it's easy to see why.

Procurement hardly owns any of the third party spend in an organization, yet if it wants to have a serious impact on spend it must address a significant portion of it. And the ownership of that spend will likely sit across several functions, geographies, or business units. If Procurement wants to make any progress, it will need the buy-in from the key people in each of those areas. In addition, C-Suite buy-in and sponsorship is required to break down possible roadblocks along the way.

So, what do we mean by buy-in?

Unfortunately, it's more complicated than simply socializing your ambition or talking through it during a kick-off meeting. In many companies, and due to the reputation of Procurement working in a silo, we have found that other functions are generally suspicious of Procurement's ambition, even if it is the right one. Many times, Procurement has pursued initiatives that appear to only be focused on something narrow, such as savings at any cost.

To get other stakeholders to buy into your Procurement ambition, they need also to understand how it aligns to their own targets. And this means CPOs need to spend significant time understanding other functions' priorities and developing their own ambition in line with those. But it doesn't even stop there.

Because Procurement has to work cross-functionally, it will need significant time and input from other functions to achieve its ambition; in particular, through requirements definition, signing off on key decisions, and providing the mandate which Procurement requires in discussions with the supply base. So, it must also secure this commitment up front from other functions too.

As we are finding, getting buy-in is not just getting an empty nod from peers for an ambition. It is about identifying the people who will be required to help Procurement achieve it, to ensure it aligns with the priorities of those people and functions, and then to secure the commitment of those people to give the time and input required throughout the journey.

This is an incredibly difficult thing to do in most businesses, especially more complex ones, and requires a high level of leadership, empathy, and networking from the CPO. We talk in more detail about these skills in Chapter 4: People. But this step is so vitally important because without buy-in, Procurement can set any ambition it likes but will never get anywhere close to achieving it.

Achieving Your Ambition: Customer Focus

Being customer focused, whether in Procurement or elsewhere, is not a new concept. It is one of those elements that when you get it right, everything else flows from it. In the end, we all exist to serve our customers, whoever they are.

If we don't have customers—people who benefit from our work and service—we won't be around for very long. They are the ones who pay our bills (directly or indirectly), who shape our approach, and who need to be kept satisfied as much as possible. But this basic concept is so often overlooked, and especially in Procurement. How many times have you looked at your Procurement function and wondered who they think they are serving, and how happy those people are with what Procurement is doing?

Procurement has historically been internally focused, but some leading functions have oriented themselves much more towards the customer recently. Despite that, in many companies, Procurement still creates processes that its customers—i.e., anyone else in the business who is trying to buy something—loathe and try to avoid. If it does any performance measurement, it usually tracks metrics that don't mean much to the rest of the business. And if it makes investments in technology, it normally does so in tools that aim to make the life of Procurement people easier, but not necessarily that of their customers.

A classic example of this is investing in an eSourcing tool. In the overwhelming majority of cases, these types of investments are targeted at helping the Procurement person to be more efficient—a noble aim, but not enough on its own. What about the business user (our customer) who profoundly dislikes the Procurement process in the first place? How is this new investment going to make a difference to them?

And why are there still some Procurement functions that are not customer focused?

It's partly because being internally focused is easier; you have much greater control over events and do not need to rely on time, input, and buy-in from others you don't directly control. And at this point we come back to ambition. In our experience the fundamental guiding principle to ensure you have a chance to achieve your Procurement ambition, once it has been set, is to be customer focused. This is about enhancing the user experience of Procurement across the business, and it will make or break your ability to achieve your ambition.

Once it has set its ambition, a pitfall for the Procurement function is to focus on itself and the tasks it needs to do without thinking how they will impact its customers. As we have discussed, a Procurement ambition cannot be achieved only by Procurement; it is a cross-functional effort, and Procurement needs to view those other functions as customers.

Some forward-thinking CPOs have taken this concept of customer focus even further. One such CPO of a large telecoms company told me once that she had long ago abandoned the idea that her Procurement function will continue to be at the center of everything, controlling how things get purchased in the wider organization. It's just not a sustainable proposition for a function that wants to provide a valuable service to its customers.

She went on, "In the pursuit of our Procurement ambition, I am constantly looking at how I can get my function out of the way. How can I make dealing with my function more and more frictionless? How can I make it easy for the business to do things for itself that my function is doing for them today? Ultimately, I'm trying to make myself redundant!" she joked. But it was only half a joke.

The moral of this story and this chapter as a whole is that achieving Procurement's ambition is not actually about Procurement. It's about Procurement's customers.

As we said at the beginning of the chapter, identifying the correct starting point and right ambition based on that starting point is critical. But in setting out to achieve that ambition, Procurement must put its customers first, and indeed the ultimate destination of any Procurement function could well be to make itself redundant.

The ambition of Procurement is not one of domination, rather it is one of service and support to other functions.

3

SOURCING EXECUTION: Making Sure That the Engine Room Delivers

Strategic Sourcing is the engine room of good Procurement and lies at the heart of maximizing its impact. However, the term is much abused and badly understood. In particular, the difference between *good* sourcing and *bad* sourcing is fundamental, and people often don't know the difference.

So, what exactly is "Strategic Sourcing?" It's not rocket science, it's really just a logical, structured, holistic way to take out large swaths of external cost. It's called a seven-step process (or similar) by the consultancies, based on Kearney's methodology developed at General Motors in the 1980s. It was a way for buyers and engineers at GM to work together to engineer and source out cost. It proved to be a winning formula, because in the GM scenario they found they could optimize the specification, and when they went out to market they had the internal customer (the engineer) on the same team and fully aligned, which improved their leverage with the suppliers. So, the magic right from Day One lay in the fact that Strategic Sourcing (or Global Sourcing, as they called it at the time) was cross-functional in nature ... the user and the commercial guy, working together to optimize the total cost of the component.

We would categorize Strategic Sourcing as: holistic (addressing the entire annualized spend and working all levers, including specifications), structured, stakeholder intensive (constant communication with, and agreement with, all key stakeholders along the way is *the* key to success), fact- and data-driven (as opposed to emotional or gut-feel-based), and cross-functional. It's also a win-win-win (Procurement, budget holder, *and* winning suppliers), rather than an exercise in beating up the suppliers.

Strategic Sourcing's objective is to keep quality and delivery at least constant, while reducing total cost of ownership. It combines a fundamental revisiting of specifications, with a well-executed supply market approach, and that's the winning combination that delivers results. As we saw in Chapter 1: Introduction, most large companies claim they're doing it but, in reality, many are not. The "Strategic Sourcing Process" diagram that follows **(see Figure 3.1)** shows a typical example. It is beyond the scope of this book to provide a step-by-step instruction manual for Strategic Sourcing, but this can be easily obtained elsewhere. Rather, we would like to bring out our key learnings over the years—in terms of what to do / what not to do, the most common pitfalls to avoid, and the key success factors.

Strategic Sourcing Process

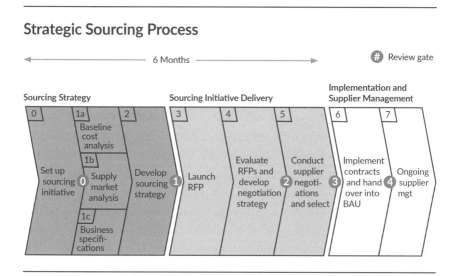

Figure 3.1   **Strategic Sourcing Process**

With that in mind, let's look briefly at each of the following summary steps: (i) building the baseline / "profiling the category"; (ii) conducting a supply market analysis; (iii) drawing up the sourcing strategy; (iv) executing an RFP event, and (v) conducting supplier negotiations and selection. Before you skip ahead … you actually *do* need to know this level of detail, despite your exalted position. With sourcing, you need to get stuck in at a nuts-and-bolts level, you can't just helicopter around the top.

Building the Baseline / "Profiling the Category"

In general, it's true that most Procurement people don't spend enough time on the early steps of building a baseline and figuring out the requirements, focusing instead on the negotiation steps at the end of the sourcing process. So, the first thing to say about the process depicted in the Strategic Sourcing Process diagram **(see Figure 3.1)** is that if you do the first few steps well, the later steps (negotiation) will fall into place much more easily, as will become apparent by the end of this chapter. If you have an excellent baseline, you have a foundation to build on; if you don't, your foundation is very weak, and this doesn't bode well.

Building the baseline or profiling the category is on the one hand about building an item level baseline of your spend in the category—understanding what you buy, in what quantities, from whom, and at what price.

On the other hand, it's about understanding and articulating (and ultimately influencing and optimizing) the business's requirements and specifications. A key priority for the Procurement person is to understand what we have in place today in the category, what the customer actually *needs*, what he/she *wants* (but doesn't truly need), what's really important to him, and what are his constraints or non-negotiables. You need to invest time with the stakeholder(s), so you can open a dialogue during which you can also open his eyes to alternative category approaches, such as outsourcing, offshoring, supplier partnering, whatever may be relevant.

The more time you spend with the budget holder early on, the better you can reflect his or her specification and needs into the sourcing process. And this is absolutely critical … that the sourcing approach is *built on* what the customer wants and needs. Otherwise, the process will implode. And this is where many Procurement efforts fail at the first hurdle. "Group solutions" are developed in a silo (e.g., "We need a global travel deal." "We should have one global laptop." etc.), and are then taken out to market without ever consulting the stakeholders.

Much of the early weeks of the sourcing team's time should be spent with the budget-holders / stakeholders. The more you can involve them in the effort the better, and the more you involve them, the more you will be sure to reflect their requirements in your sourcing strategy.

You need to take your stakeholders on a *journey*, because it takes time to change people's positions or open their minds. It's very reward-ing when stakeholders do open up—suddenly they're not as attached to their "pet supplier," suddenly they're working collaboratively to pool their spend with other business units, rather than being defensive. And 90% of the time, this change does occur—a little fact and a little persuasiveness can go a long way.

So, use the baselining stage to get close to the internal customer and to make sure you can fully articulate their needs to the supply mar-ket. That's the "soft" part of the equation; the "hard" part is getting the data part right. We're talking line-item level, by supplier, with price, quantity, drawing / specification … the whole nine yards. But that data is critical—the quality of your baseline data will significantly impact the rest of the sourcing effort, not least because of how you come across with internal stakeholders.

If you have complete and accurate baseline data, then you will impress … you will be bringing something to the table, which imme-diately puts you in a good spot with your stakeholders. I won't go into how to build a category baseline in detail here, but I will say the fol-lowing: (i) allow enough time, four to six weeks, and don't accept a "quick-and-dirty"; (ii) put someone competent and resilient on the job, because it's not easy; (iii) tap the suppliers for line item data rather than your internal systems … it's almost always the easier way to go; and (iv) teach your people to present the data and to synthesize the "So what?" … having a database with 18,000 price points is of no use to me if you can't tell me what it means. And don't be tempted to cut corners when building your baseline … it will cost you dearly in the subsequent steps of the process.

One final point on baselining: in estimating your future volumes, don't just look to the past! Sure, next year's spend, in most categories, will be based on last year's spend. But there will be adjustments, and you can factor those in: volume reductions due to the sale of a business unit, for example. More importantly, factor in your future *growth*. For categories like Software, Cloud Computing, Construction, and Facilities Management (FM), a forward-looking forecast is vitally important.

Conducting a Supply Market Analysis

This is a relatively minor step in the process, but it's one that's often not done well. Most sourcing processes would require a supply market analysis to be performed in parallel to the internal baselining, so that *both* can inform the subsequent step, the sourcing strategy. However, despite the fact that we live in an age of information ubiquity, many Procurement functions do the "supply market analysis" step no justice.

This is where "tick box best practice" comes in … yes, we've done a supply market analysis, and here is the presentation. First slide: a pie chart showing how the global market for IT Hardware breaks down by continent, and then a line graph showing 4% market growth over the last few years … so … what does this tell us?

The point is, more often than not, a supply market study is done for the sake of ticking a box, and in no way informs the sourcing strategy. What it *should* be doing instead is asking intelligent questions about how buyers and suppliers do business. How are our competitors buying the category? Is there a different contracting model emerging in the market that would benefit us? What do my suppliers' cost structures look like, and would they benefit from significant incremental volume? Should we be buying from distributors and also negotiating trilaterally with OEMs for "A items?" Should we take advantage of new capacity emerging in India?

Best practice is to start with hypotheses that need to be tested and proven / disproven. "Suppliers will give large discounts for incremental volume. Test."; "It makes sense to buy directly from the manufacturers in China rather than from the European distributors, who apply excessive mark-ups. Test."; "Outsourcing our in-house metal parts Manufacturing operations would yield significant benefits. Test."

Research is there for one reason: to inform, to answer a question; make sure your supply market analysis does so.

And please do make sure that your supply market research has the question, "What are the supplier's needs and wants, and what's in it for them?" front and center. There is probably something you can give your suppliers for which they will provide you with a healthy saving.

I remember sourcing Engine Testing for a Big Five auto OEM comprised of a number of car brands. Towards the end of the product development process, an engine had to be shipped to a "test bed," a rig that holds an engine and runs it for thousands of hours while taking a myriad of diagnostic readings. The test bed suppliers were the automotive engineering companies, for whom the test beds were a frustrating side business—very high fixed costs, very dependent on bed utilization ... a hotel for engines!

The suppliers were dealing with the client's various car brands, none of which by themselves had a sizeable or predictable volume. But when we put the volumes of the six brands together, we realized we had more than two-thirds of the top two suppliers' capacity tied up. So, we guaranteed them a minimum of 50% utilization per annum, plus frequent and accurate demand forecasting. Of course, they jumped at the chance of, in one fell swoop, getting rid of at least half of the utilization headache, and we saved the client 35% annually—all based on empathizing with the supplier's high fixed cost base and using it to our, and to their, advantage.

Above all else, make sure that your teams are actually talking to the suppliers, both incumbent and non-incumbent, during this stage of the sourcing process. This is absolutely vital—in the end, "a deal will be done" between your organizations and one or several of theirs—so let's make sure we understand their business and what they want and need. In organizations where an old school, strong-arm Procurement culture still exists, the tendency is *not* to talk to suppliers, because it is seen as a weakness. Nothing could be further from the truth.

Your suppliers most likely understand the category better than you do, and they're usually champing at the bit to bring their improvement ideas to the table. This needs to be harnessed. Nothing brings a sourcing team up the learning curve more quickly than a "supplier day" early in the sourcing process, in which a handful of major incumbent and non-incumbent suppliers are invited to come and speak to the sourcing team about their market, the different contracting models that exist, best practices they've seen at other clients, and their ideas for improvements and cost reductions at the client company. A day spent this way will catapult the team up the learning curve.

Drawing Up the Sourcing Strategy

Essentially, the internal baseline / profile, when combined with the supply market analysis, should lead to the sourcing strategy. They should *point to* a set of sourcing strategies; and when you present said sourcing strategy, the baseline and market analysis need to explain and legitimize it.

The sourcing strategy needs to encompass the full range of value levers appropriate to the category. All consultancies peddle a version of "the six generic sourcing strategies" or the "sourcing diamond," and even a "Procurement chess board." In reality, very often the only Procurement strategy used is "coming in at the last minute to negotiate the price a little and then sign the contract." The Six Generic Sourcing Strategies diagram that follows (see **Figure 3.2**) depicts the range of sourcing levers available, distinguishing between "supply side" (where the suppliers generate the saving) and "demand side" (where *you* generate the saving).

As a bare minimum, make sure you "go around the wheel" and brainstorm how each strategy may or may not apply to your category. What you often find is that yes, you can leverage the supply market, but there's not much point until you've done some "demand side" clean-up. For example, if sourcing Pipes, Valves and Fittings, how much more interesting would your spend be to those suppliers if you consolidated it first, so that you're no longer buying 7,500 SKUs but 500?

Other categories are *all* about the demand side levers. Take Factory Cleaning. If you have five factories in five locations and they require X hours of cleaning each per week, then appointing a single supplier is not going to yield any scale effects. Yet how often have I seen Cleaning

Six Generic Sourcing Strategies

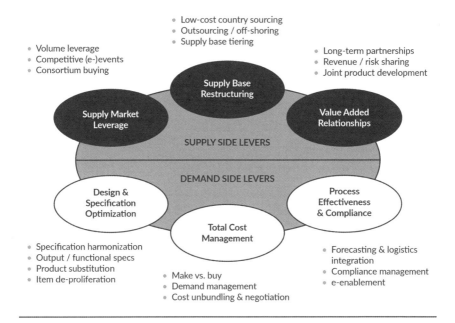

Figure 3.2 Six Generic Sourcing Strategies

sourcing strategies involving "pooling volume" and "consolidating suppliers." That's all dandy, but it won't give you any savings; cleaning is pretty much *all* about labor productivity, which in turn is *all* about the spec. So, when we're drawing up the sourcing strategy, let's be sure to look at all the levers, but then focus on the relevant ones for the category.

The strategies depicted in the previous diagram **(see Figure 3.2)** are not rocket science in themselves but, if applied intelligently and in combination, they can work to fundamentally reset the cost base of the category. And yet many C-Suite executives don't understand or accept that Procurement's remit stretches to the demand levers. But it absolutely needs to … half of all sourcing savings will come from addressing and harmonizing the specifications of what you're buying. So, to just "take out to market the same thing we've always bought" is less than half the story. You need to be going after specification and process change, changing *what* is bought and *how* it's bought, rather than just *at what price* it's bought.

Adopting a holistic approach also means that the commercial model with the supplier is up for debate: Are we stuck with unit costs for materials and an hourly rate for labor? Or can we combine the materials and a fixed number of hours into a fixed cost per unit of output? Beyond this, can we share in any savings with the supplier?

I remember sourcing mobile phone base stations for a telecom operator during the roll-out of 3G (shows my age!). We started with a simple bill of materials price list used in the design and construction of each base station. We then moved to bidding base stations out in geographic groups, so that supplier scale economies could be leveraged. In the end, we had so many data points that we fixed the price per base station—each one was different, but we used our experience to statistically determine a safe fixed price, thereby massively reducing the administrative burden associated with each site during the latter stages of the build-out.

On top of that, we incentivized the suppliers to come in below the fixed price, by sharing the resulting savings with them. Interestingly, both of these new commercial models (site bundles, fixed price) were suggested by the suppliers, who had been busy building huge numbers of base stations for other operators. The project was a runaway success that generated significant savings during the client's 3G roll-out and was praised widely by the industry.

Executing an RFP Event

An RFP (Request for Proposal) is a powerful vehicle for getting the lion's share of the sourcing strategy implemented in one go. As soon as people read "RFP," they read "a vehicle for beating up suppliers," but nothing could be further from the truth. The RFP process should take to market *your newly defined requirements*. An RFP is very powerful, because it allows you to access both supply and demand levers with one vehicle. The bad news is, the requirement actually needs to be re-defined and fully articulated first, before the RFP can go out.

So, once the sourcing strategy is signed off, in all likelihood, the team will go out to the market with an RFP. But they may not.

In some instances, an RFP-based competitive process is not workable or appropriate, for example when dealing with monopolistic suppliers. An RFP is not *always* the answer … however, because it fosters competition amongst suppliers, it's by far the preferred route if you have the option of taking it.

If you have to run a process *without* an RFP, it's key that you still build a credible challenge / threat / opportunity for the supplier. Without an RFP, this is much more difficult to do, and will likely require (i) a strong supply market understanding to unearth benchmarks and insights that you can use as leverage in lieu of RFP insights, and (ii) a sophisticated should-cost model (instead of competitor price points).

A non-competitive approach also requires even more alignment with your stakeholders—you can't use competing suppliers to create pressure, so you need to use your internal stakeholders instead. Whichever way you look at it, an RFP is just easier, because it engenders competition, and because it effectively outsources much of the work of sourcing to the suppliers … and those suppliers are keen to participate, so the work gets done!

As a consultant, I've participated in hundreds of RFPs as a supplier. I can tell you, the quality of the RFP invitation documentation we receive is, in general, quite poor. The RFP needs to do a number of things, not just obtain a quote from the supplier. It needs to set out the opportunity and make it exciting and tangible for the supplier.

Procurement is not just about stick, it's also about carrot. Yes, you have to *sell* yourself and your organization, you have to make them want you. So, you need to tell the competing suppliers: the size of your spend, the projected size of your spend in five years' time, given your growth strategy, the current allocation of that spend across suppliers, and the allocation to be. In other words, "We spend $100m across 63 suppliers. We aim to go to a small group of three to four primary suppliers for 75% of that volume." Then the suppliers can see, there is for them an opportunity of up to $25m. If you want them to sharpen their pencils, you've got to make it worth their while.

The RFP is your opportunity to (i) pique the market's interest, and (ii) show the suppliers that you're serious, both of which are very much in your interest. So why on earth would you send the tender documentation unannounced by email to your local sales rep?

A much better solution is to invite the sales directors of the suppliers to an RFP launch event, at which the RFP will be presented and explained. This has a number of advantages: (i) the suppliers get to lay eyes on their competition, which is always good; (ii) you can fully lay out your strategy and articulate the supplier carrot; ideally in fact, you should have the budget-holder executive from your company give the opening address; and (iii) you can explain in detail how you need the RFP filled in—walk them through the spreadsheet, it will save your team a lot of time by minimizing mistakes, questions, and re-work.

A primary objective of the RFP launch event should be to convey your seriousness of intent to the suppliers. Suppliers are often skeptical about "Procurement exercises," having seen too many examples of being promised big changes, and then nothing happening in reality, apart from their pricing being squeezed. If you can show them that you have a clear strategy, and, most importantly, that you are aligned with the budget-holder, then half the battle is won.

Beyond this, the RFP obviously needs to be well thought-through, and solicit all the relevant information in a format that can be easily compared across bidders. The qualitative questionnaire should cover specific, relevant questions only, and should be easy to answer / fill out and analyze (no essays, please). The pricing response sheet is critically important. The prices need to be comparable across suppliers, and they need to be comparable to your baseline prices … if they don't map, you need to find a way of mapping them. And the pricing needs to be as unbundled as possible.

In Strategic Sourcing, negotiations are based on providing suppliers feedback after you've analyzed and compared their bids. For example, "Your cost per unit is 25% higher than the best bidders. Your labor costs are fine, but it seems to take you 23% more hours per part than the average bidder. You may want to reconsider your bid in light of this information." So, in the RFP response, you're looking for granular, comparable metrics that you can use to inform the supplier that their bid is not competitive. And the more you can take those metrics down to a cost component level ("your cost of resin seems way off"), then you're giving the supplier something they can take back to their organization and work with.

A final word on RFPs: while the RFP is active, you have a huge amount of tension amongst the suppliers. You must capitalize on this to get as much agreed with the suppliers as possible before your leverage evaporates, which happens the minute you announce the winners. Too many companies make the mistake of picking the winning supplier, and *then* start to think about transitioning in the supplier. Instead, get the transition plan (and the full contract!) agreed with the supplier first. *Then* let them know they've won.

There is a tendency these days, in some quarters of the Procurement community, to "pooh-pooh" the use of RFPs. I've heard consultants referred to as "tender monkeys"—because it's unintelligent work, they just crank the handle on the big tender machine. Our view is that these detractors don't understand the role, and value, of a powerful RFP. It's a unifying tool that, if used properly, gets the attention of the market, assembles a huge amount of powerful data in minimal time, and provides the basis for a highly informed and very fruitful negotiation … without the need for banging fists on tables!

Conducting Supplier Negotiations and Selection

The more effort you put into designing the RFP, the easier your negotiations will be. In fact, if you have a strong baseline and a coherent strategy, you can show to the suppliers a credible threat and carrot, and you can convey to them that you have the stakeholder functions behind you, then the suppliers will typically be more than amenable.

The next diagram (see Figure 3.3) conceptually shows the key success factors of sourcing, and how getting each step right makes the subsequent steps more powerful. Armed with a strong baseline and a thorough understanding of the suppliers' wants and needs, you can develop a workable strategy and present a compelling business case for change, which in turn enables you to gain stakeholder buy-in, which in turn allows you to develop a very strong RFP, with clear and credible "carrots and sticks." This in turn unlocks the negotiations and the ultimate result.

Strategic Sourcing Success Factors

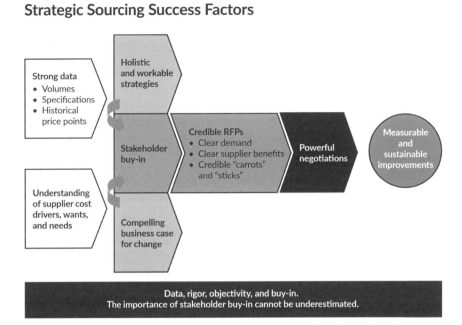

Figure 3.3   Strategic Sourcing Success Factors

Conversely ... get the early steps, the data gathering, and the supply market research *wrong* ... and you won't be able to build a solid strategy or benefits case, so the stakeholders will be lukewarm. The suppliers will sense this and reflect it in their proposals accordingly.

We won't try to cram a course on negotiating into this book—there are plenty of good books on that subject already. But it's worth quickly describing how Strategic Sourcing negotiations work.

There are typically three rounds of negotiation that build on each other. The first meeting is to clarify the RFP response and inform the supplier of where they stand competitively (without of course revealing other suppliers' bids as such)—to show them where they "have work to do" if they want to proceed. There are then typically two further rounds. At each round, the supplier is pushed further. Where the early rounds focus more on the non-commercial elements (to weed out the low-capability players early in the process), subsequent rounds should focus more on the commercials.

The aim is to make all the suppliers as commercially competitive as possible, or as they are willing to be, and to then make a choice. Suppliers should be plotted on a dynamic matrix of Capability versus Commercials, with the aim of making the most competent suppliers' bids as attractive as possible. The choice is then ultimately a trade-off between capability and cost—and the solution that optimizes both to the greatest degree possible is the winner. It's worth noting that it's far from mandatory to pick the cheapest supplier—you might go for a 10% saving with the most capable supplier, despite the offer of a 13% saving from a less capable player.

What's interesting is that the suppliers who participate in well-executed Strategic Sourcing processes often contact us to express their appreciation. They are big fans of the feedback approach ... because it's useful to them. It shows them, in a fact-based and non-emotional manner, how their bid stacks up, and where they can improve (both in capability and in price) versus the competition. When you think about it, that makes sense.

Who wouldn't want to know, for example, how their costs in their five or six biggest cost buckets compare to those of their competitors? What great intelligence, and it's free! Yes, you want to leverage your power in a negotiation ... but it's much more powerful to do so by letting the facts speak for you than by pounding your fist on the table. It's more powerful, it's more respectful, it's more collaborative, and it gets a better result. Strategic Sourcing is not about being a tough guy, it's about using data and facts to drive towards your optimum position.

After a very quick tour of key dos and don'ts during each step of the sourcing process, let's look at a couple of other topics, focusing at the entire process rather than the sub-steps.

Sourcing Tools

"Should I be using e-sourcing and e-auctions to get the best result?" I hear you ask. Absolutely, but (i) only buy the tools you need, and make sure you actually use them; and (ii) don't try to run before you can walk. I've seen so many organizations that had only a very limited Procurement capability, declare that, henceforth, everything must be bought through an e-sourcing platform, and the result is predictable. You can't automate a poor process and expect it to be any better.

The sourcing tools available in the market are improving day by day. There are all manner of tools available, but in the context of Strategic Sourcing we're mainly talking e-auctions and e-sourcing. E-auctions are interesting: they're less a technology and more a form of negotiation. Today they have found their place in life as being one of a range of potential approaches (or tools) that one may or may not apply, and they can be used as the primary bidding mechanism, or they can be part of a broader RFP exercise. E-auctions can be very effective, but our recommendation is to use them as part of a toolbox rather than as a standard approach.

E-sourcing tools, or e-RFX tools, aim to facilitate the entire bidding process, by allowing you to post your tender using an online portal that bidders then access to place their bids. The early versions of e-sourcing arguably managed to make the whole process *less* slick than it was before, but today's tools are much more user-friendly.

A key consideration with e-sourcing tools is how the pricing is managed—it can be easiest to append the pricing sheets in Excel, unless the e-sourcing tool has a sophisticated and easily configurable pricing module. A further consideration is category specificity—the way categories are bid out varies tremendously, and a one-size solution can be difficult to adapt to the needs of each category.

The future likely lies in "intelligent" category-specific e-sourcing tools that are designed around the optimum category strategy and come preloaded with a category-specific pricing sheet and pricing analysis tool, as well as capability questions that can be amended as required for each situation.

Software in itself is not the solution; if it is combined with high quality content however, then you have something that can really enhance the capabilities of your buyers.

Savings Credibility

Savings are the topic of another chapter of this book (Chapter 9: Savings Realization). What is relevant during sourcing is that (i) there is a dedicated Finance "implant" working on the program, and

(ii) that person works with all the sourcing teams from baseline to savings sign-off, thus ensuring that the numbers are accurate, and that we know with great certainty what are today's costs and what are tomorrow's costs with our new pricing in place. At the end of the process, each sourcing team needs to formally have their expected savings signed off by Finance, and the budget-holder needs to agree.

Sourcing Gates

Another key success factor is the establishment of formal "gates" throughout the sourcing process, whereby a team can only proceed to the next step of the process upon receiving formal sign-off for their baseline, their strategy, the RFP, the bidders' list, and so on. It's very difficult for a stakeholder to wriggle out of signing the deal at the last minute, if he / she has already signed off on the baseline, the specification, the RFP, and the negotiating strategy. Buy-in doesn't come quickly, or in one go; it comes bit by bit, step by step, so that by the end of the process, there is little left to question. It pays to formalize this step-by-step approach to getting agreement, through the establishment of sourcing gates.

Time with Stakeholders

Key to the success of sourcing is that you spend a lot of *time* with the people from the budget-holder functions. This is *their* spend, and they need to be fully involved in developing the specification, writing the RFP, determining what suppliers do and don't get invited to bid … this requires a lot of time and patience.

When you see "group deals" that nobody buys into in the country business units, it's because they were never consulted about what was important to them, who they were currently buying from and why, what would persuade them to look at other options, and so on. Spend time with your stakeholders, show them you care, and try to impress them. If you bring them quality (a quality baseline, a great RFP draft, a comprehensive supplier list, an insightful analysis of price bids), then you will get them on your side. Do the right thing and do it well, and the rest will follow.

But the stakeholders themselves must also play their part. In particular, the C-Suite has an obligation to champion the Procurement effort. They need to be engaged, and they need to challenge the team. They need to be asking tough questions, like "Why is this a strategic supplier that we can't go after?," "When you say we tried off-shoring before but the numbers didn't stack up, is it because our numbers weren't very good?," and "How are we going to get those big IT vendors to take this tender seriously?"

The C-Suite needs to *actively* champion the Procurement effort ... relentlessly removing roadblocks and helping to seize opportunities.

Program Management

Strategic Sourcing needs to be run like a program—high energy, good people, truly cross-functional engagement ... otherwise it doesn't work! You can't just get the Accenture Category Sourcing Process and off you go.

First and foremost, the project needs to be structured properly, which means cross-functionally at every level—from the sourcing teams to the Executive Steering Committee. And it's not just about "having representation from Marketing," but having those folks fully invested in the effort, and even ideally leading some of the sourcing teams.

A sourcing program should *not* be a Procurement-driven effort. You must do it *with* the budget-holders, not *to* them, and so there should be a structured, fully cross-functional Program org chart that includes the Steering Committee, the Project Management Office (which includes the Finance implant), and the sourcing teams, as shown in the next diagram (see **Figure 3.4**).

Beyond this, it's worth stressing that sourcing program management must be *content-driven* rather than process-driven. That is to say, it needs to be focused on the nuts-and-bolts of the operational sourcing work and, more specifically, on removing nuts-and-bolts obstacles for the sourcing teams. The drumbeat and the momentum of the program can only be maintained if the obstacles that will endlessly arise can be quickly and effectively removed. That's the job of the Program Office, and this position needs to be staffed by one of your best people.

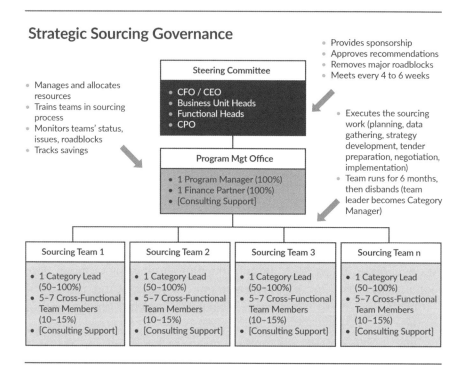

Figure 3.4   Strategic Sourcing Governance

Execution

We're at the end of the chapter, and we've not yet talked about the other word in the chapter's title, the word "execution." Or have we? Have we actually been talking about nothing more than good old-fashioned execution in this chapter? Because the point about sourcing is that it's all about good execution. If sourcing is well executed, it's very powerful, but often those executing it lack the time, skills, motivation, and incentives to do it well. The result is a house built on poor foundations … hence the reason why so many "savings" later fail to materialize.

So, what is good execution all about? It's about all the little things … making sure you've consulted with everyone, making sure your numbers and analyses stack up, communicating your strategy well, and orchestrating meetings so that decisions get made and stuff gets implemented.

All your "products"—spend analysis, supply market analysis, category strategy, RFI, RFP, bid evaluation mechanism ... all these things—need to be of the highest quality. And that still doesn't guarantee success.

Beyond the basics, it's about working well, and respectfully, with colleagues from other functions. It's the difference between a terrible supplier bidder list and an excellent supplier bidder list. And execution is about intelligence—if the approach you're advocating is a smart move, and you're smart about articulating it and getting everyone on board, then you will get it done. Good execution is a mix of being smart, being pragmatic, being pushy but respectful, and selling yourself well. Not an easy ask—but that's why really good execution is so rare ... it requires multi-talented people.

After the Storm

The suppliers have been selected, the savings have been signed off, let's pack our bags and go home. Wrong! There is a major disconnect that exists in the majority of organizations that this book's authors have seen, and that is that Procurement pulls out and hands the category back to the budget-holder too soon.

Procurement needs to stay involved with the category ongoing, not just during the sourcing event. This means managing the suppliers through quarterly meetings, and it means monitoring compliance. "Supplier Relationship Management" doesn't exist in most companies, because it falls between two stools, with neither Procurement nor the budget-holder taking responsibility for it.

And, of course, you can't rest on your laurels just because the sourcing was successful. Sourcing needs to be followed up by year-on-year savings in the order of 2% to 3%, and these will only come through proactive engagement of the suppliers in the identification of incremental efficiency opportunities.

Sourcing Is the Engine Room

At the end of the day, sourcing underlies everything we do in Procurement. It's how we add value, it's how we make savings, it's how we're viewed by the rest of the business. It needs to be structured, holistic, data-driven, tightly managed, cross-functional, empowered, and of the highest quality. Then the CPO will shine, the savings will be co-owned by the budget-holder, the sourcing solutions will be good for the customer ... and your chosen suppliers will be happy! Do sourcing badly, on the other hand, and you're a laughingstock across the organization.

And it ain't rocket science. Good Strategic Sourcing is mostly about just executing well. Executing an intelligent, well-managed, holistic yet focused, data-driven, and stakeholder input-intensive process to optimize the total cost of a category of external spend.

Strategic Sourcing. It's been around for a while so everyone thinks they can do it but, in reality, relatively few do it really well. It's getting long-in-the-tooth, but it's still the key to unlocking the power of Procurement; it's still the engine room. It should be what makes up most of the work of your strategic buyers, because it's what generates that critical EBITDA value.

And that, in the end, is what it's all about.

4

PEOPLE: Building a Winning Procurement Team

Who Do We Need in Procurement?

When evaluating the maturity and potential of the Procurement function, a simple shortcut to the answer is to look at its people. How much do you trust them? How often do you see them? And are they understood by the rest of the business? While some companies perform well here, the answers can be the same for others: not much.

Procurement functions don't always comprise the top talent in the company. Part of this is because Procurement has its roots as an administrative function with a constrained remit, as discussed in Chapter 1: Introduction. Which high potential, career-hungry person would choose a position in Procurement if other functions such as Sales, Marketing, or Finance have a more central role in value delivery for their organization?

The problem is compounded because we sometimes don't know what type of people to hire in Procurement, so we just end up hiring those with the word "Procurement" on their CV. And this can reinforce the problem. But there are exceptions. One CPO told me last year that he routinely rejects people who apply to their Procurement team with "fantastic Procurement resumes," not because they are bad people, but because the skills are too "old school."

The CPO

Before we get into defining old school Procurement skills, let's talk about who is needed at the head of the function. In this case, we're calling them the CPO, but they could be called Procurement Director, Head of Procurement, or even Procurement Manager depending on the size of the firm. Actually, the title CPO is a bit misleading here because the "C" is generally associated with a board-level position that Procurement doesn't normally occupy.

It has long been a topic of debate in Procurement as to whether the CPO should be on the board but, in our experience, having Procurement representation on the board doesn't make much difference in terms of how effective it can be. Why? Because a good CPO is someone with excellent stakeholder engagement skills, someone who has built strong relationships with key people and who empathizes well with them—including all board members. For some companies, Procurement is a board position—particularly where Procurement is so business-critical, such as automotive—but for others not, and Procurement shouldn't get too worked up about it, either way. If the CPO possesses the right skills, he or she will have access to every board member every day of the week anyway.

A key part of being able to play the role we've just described is an ability to talk the language of the business. How many functional heads' eyes glaze over if the CPO starts talking about savings that no one recognizes, processes that no one wants, or a supplier deal that sounds overly complicated? Good CPOs, and there are many out there, understand the business priorities first and then make the link between what they want to talk about and why the rest of the company should care—in a language that others can understand.

Another essential trait is the ability to constructively challenge others on the status quo. Have you ever seen your CPO battling with their peers on the nuances of a position? Were you impressed? Some CPOs struggle to challenge effectively, partly because they talk the wrong language but also because they can lack the confidence and insight to do so. But challenge is what a CPO must do, because they need to be the ones in the organization sparking and then driving change.

Finally, a CPO needs to be comfortable existing to make others more effective. It's not a secret that CPOs can sometimes find themselves in conflict with other functions and working in a silo. But Procurement must help other functions meet their targets, and it needs to be relentless in its cross-functional approach to do so. Some of the best CPOs we have had the pleasure of seeing in action look for ways to get their function out of the way of the business to allow the business to do it themselves! That calls for a level of humility and shared purpose.

Today's Old School Procurement Skillset

So, what is this old school Procurement skillset that you still find in some companies today? Well, part of it is completing tasks like updating master data records by liaising with the business and suppliers and trying to ensure policies and procedures are followed by people who don't want to follow them. As you can imagine, this type of process policeman role doesn't really endear Procurement people to their colleagues in other functions. Procurement processes are notoriously long-winded and have a reputation for not being designed with the end user in mind.

The second is that some Procurement functions are not in control of their agenda or program of work. Instead, they are overwhelmed trying to react to issues and requests being raised by the business and suppliers that come up last minute. Since when did working in a reactive fashion and on mainly administrative tasks require highly talented people? Not being very liked and spending so much time on the back foot takes its toll such that many Procurement people who spend their days doing this day in and day out, are generally worn down. Therefore, in these cases, they show little ambition to make their roles more fulfilling and valuable to the company. That is not to say these people are not in general hard-working, they often are! But they and their Procurement functions are in a rut that is hard to get out of.

As with many things, the talent issue in Procurement stems from a lack of understanding of what Procurement can deliver and therefore the sort of people needed and the qualifications required. This creates a low bar and explains why you can end up with people in Procurement roles who are behind their peers in, say, the Engineering function, or the Sales function, in which certain qualifications and standards are required. Just look at the ratio of degree-educated people in the Procurement team compared to, say, Finance. It's pretty revealing! The people in these other functions are sometimes more capable and therefore exert considerable influence over their colleagues in Procurement, often taking ownership of strategic tasks that overlap with Procurement such as liaising with suppliers on important topics and making commercial decisions with Procurement expected to fall into line.

Of course, there are many exceptions to this and plenty of highly educated and very effective people out there in Procurement who do incredible things for their companies. Believe us, we have come across many of them! But we think there is a big opportunity to make this more common across more companies than it is today.

As already mentioned, what *does* sometimes seem to be valued by companies in their Procurement teams is "Procurement experience." You just need look at the number of Procurement job adverts out there that make this a prerequisite. If you question what is meant by this, you'll often get a vague answer about it meaning good process knowledge, or similar. Actually, we think it can in some cases betray a lack of understanding of what actual skills should be sought.

A large part of Procurement's role today is about ensuring that due process is followed—usually a complex sourcing or contracting process, complete with heavy forms to fill in. Another skill that some companies genuinely appear to value today is the knowledge that a Procurement professional has of categories and key suppliers and even the individual day-to-day relationships they have with supplier counterparts. This is particularly interesting, and our experience in consulting shows that our clients often want our consultants to have massive amounts of supplier and market knowledge.

However, this doesn't make the difference between success and failure in Procurement, at least not always. One of the large pharma companies has recognized this and has started to post actual problem statements that they have in their business in place of traditional job descriptions. They then hire those people who can help them solve these problems, regardless of any Procurement experience.

Finally, some companies prioritize good negotiation skills. But negotiation skills as defined—as they often are in this context—by being able to navigate the theatrics of a series of negotiations with a supplier and score a win by getting the lowest unit price, without taking into account other factors, are in fact grossly overrated. By being more data-driven and striving for longer term win-win deals with suppliers, it is possible to get far superior results without all the emotion and theatrics.

Tomorrow's Procurement Team

We've had the good fortune of working with many high-performing CPOs and the teams they have built over the years and, from this experience, we have summarized a list of four principles that any CPO should consider when putting his or her team together to ensure success from the start. These principles depart from some of the traditional approaches we have just examined that some companies still follow. They are:

- Define success and align incentives,
- Build a team of diverse skills,
- Ensure the team is versatile,
- Focus on execution.

Define success and align incentives

In the best Procurement departments, we have seen the people who can say clearly how their personal objectives and incentives align to the broader objectives of the function in which they work. But this is not true in all companies.

Consider the Sales function of any company. Most people will have personal sales targets that make up part of the overall company sales target. Delivery or customer services teams often have clear customer satisfaction goals which cascade down to account directors and managers in those teams. And, in most cases, product teams have market share and sales targets that are shared amongst the employees. Everyone in the team is working to the same goal and individuals know how their role contributes. Such clear objectives allow effective incentivization, whether financial or otherwise, and it enables teams to perform at the highest level. There is no reason why Procurement should be exempt from this but in some companies it seems to be.

A fundamental part of building an effective Procurement team is firstly to define the objectives of the Procurement function clearly, how success against that is going to be measured, and then get buy-in from peers and management. This last step is critical. Some Procurement functions will say they have a target but, ask others outside of Procurement who should know what that target is, they invariably say that they don't.

The targets will differ by business, but a common objective will be savings; another could be supplier performance or perhaps supply chain risk reduction, or some combination. The point is to define the objective. Defining success metrics must then follow. For example, if savings is the overriding objective how are they going to be measured? Do OpEx and CapEx savings have the same value in the business? Once this is done, ensure that the targets do not conflict with other functions' targets and, even better, enlist their support in helping you to reach yours.

Taking the time to get clarity on objectives and success measures and socializing these then allows the CPO to break up and cascade these targets to teams and individuals within Procurement, also providing options on incentivization. This will help you get the most from your people. It also ensures people in the Procurement team can work harmoniously with people in other teams, since targets align.

Build a team of diverse skills

It is not possible to describe the ideal Procurement professional, so that is not what we will do. In today's environment, a Procurement function needs to have a broad skillset at its disposal. This starts with analytical and commercial skills.

Analytical skills are more than being good with Excel, being able to program formulae, and being good at arithmetic, although all that certainly helps. A high-performing Procurement team needs people with an ability to absorb and leverage insight to create actions, spark interest, and give a feel for opportunities, being able to compare and assess supplier proposals and unpick them, and spot the right elements that make it a good or a bad one. Some people spend most of their day doing analytics that never result in anything actionable—unless there is an action, the analysis is a waste of time.

Commercial skills, on the other hand, link to an instinct to where there is more in a deal, to have a good feel for elements that will improve it or make it less risky, and playing the right timing for specific asks—not too early, not too late—making suppliers believe the ask. Note, this is different to how we defined traditional negotiation skills earlier in the chapter, which was more about being poker-faced and then exploding in a supplier discussion for maximum effect.

To complement such impressive analytical and commercial skills in the Procurement function, however, also requires that the team possesses individuals with excellent people and stakeholder management skills. Procurement is as much about driving change than anything else, and it doesn't matter if your expert analysis shows a clear opportunity. Unless you have people who can bring the rest of the business along on the journey, the journey won't happen. It's surprising how a compelling analysis can be stopped in its tracks because people upon whom Procurement relies to make the change happen either mistrust the motive of the proposed change or harbor concerns about potential consequences.

So, what makes a good stakeholder manager? Firstly, these people require empathy and understand the importance of getting others to trust them. As we said before, they are able to speak to others in their language—and by that we mean corporate / functional language—so that they can buy into the change and journey. You need people who take the time to plan and run status or update meetings with their internal customers, and who also take the time to build informal relationships with key stakeholders.

Of course, there is a need for administrative work in Procurement, but this needs to be kept away from those with advanced analytical and commercial skills and the highly developed soft skills that we've just described. Segregating the team like this ensures the top talent in Procurement can focus on the task of bringing value to the organization unencumbered by administrative tasks. This is vital, because it is these tasks that can often feel like the most urgent, even if they are not important; so, unless there are clear lines drawn, the whole team can be dragged into them.

Ensure the team is versatile

Traditionally, people in Procurement have tended to have quite fixed roles, even those resources who would be classed as strategic and do fewer administrative tasks. For example, there might be a category manager who looks after IT spend and has relationships with the IT stakeholders, and then there is a category manager who focuses on Marketing and only works with the Marketing team. One key drawback to this is that it does not reflect the huge peaks and troughs of work that most businesses experience in Procurement activity caused by large projects or ever-changing priorities.

A retail bank recently embarked upon a significant upgrading of its IT infrastructure to better service its customers, and this added huge strain to the IT category manager because of their very rigid Procurement team structure. They didn't pull in other category managers from the wider Procurement team to help, partly because those other ones didn't view it as their role, even when some of those people weren't busy. Global events like COVID-19 amplify this need to be versatile as business priorities change in an instant. During such times, the versatile teams will win.

What is needed is an agile pool of project managers in Procurement that can, and are willing to, go where the need is greatest. And this is where the analytical, commercial, and soft skills are so valuable, because they are transferable across any spend type and any set of stakeholders.

A large utility company in the UK is close to perfecting this model. They have two dozen people in the Procurement team and while the most senior are affiliated to categories, mainly from an accountability perspective, it's only a loose affiliation. The rest of the team goes where the priority is, and it works brilliantly. The priorities are addressed, and there is variation for the team.

One of the arguments sometimes given against this approach is that people who work across different categories can't possibly hold category-specific knowledge for each one. However, in our experience, category specific knowledge is not, in general, near the top of the list of value contributions Procurement can make to a sourcing project. Most of the knowledge already resides with the stakeholders and suppliers and, where there are gaps, it does not take long or cost much to speak to a genuine expert, who can be external, and get what you need from them.

For large spend areas, in which there will be a guarantee of constant Procurement involvement, having someone with specialist market knowledge in the Procurement team can work, as long as that person is deployed wisely. That means making sure they spend most of their time imparting their knowledge to others doing the project work. That is different to being busy themselves with project work, with no time to help others by imparting their knowledge.

This versatile approach is in general more appealing to the type of people who have the desired profile for Procurement that we've talked about. These are typically people with a thirst for new challenges, people who are intellectually curious, and who enjoy working with different stakeholders. It's therefore also a key part of keeping your best people challenged and motivated. More about that a little later in this chapter.

Focus on execution

Finally, all Procurement teams need a relentless focus on high quality execution. Most Procurement functions have defined processes, albeit not always accessible and sometimes many versions of the truth. However, how many really execute those processes well?

Procurement processes shouldn't even be particularly complicated in the sense that the steps ought to be clear. Take the seven-step sourcing process that has been around for decades. One of the first steps is to build a category baseline, which is an understanding of the spend of the category. The level of detail required will depend on the criticality of the category to the business, but even those companies that deploy seven-step sourcing will not always complete the step well. The spend profile they come up with may be incomplete, inaccurate, not detailed enough … the list goes on.

In building the best team, you need to have people who can execute well. This is about creating the right output that is high quality, consistently. And, to do this, a Procurement team needs people who are customer-focused, who care about what they do, and who are structured and logical. That is more important than having people who know the process, which is generally easy to pick up. The best Procurement teams have people who understand what their internal customers want and ensure they get it—even when that involves going the extra mile. This, in turn, creates more of a pull for Procurement's services and elevates the function.

As well as simply having people who are great at executing, ensuring that there are ways in the team to share practices and learn from each other is just as important. Being able to execute well is something that can be learned, and through knowledge-sharing forums and informal coaching the standard of execution across the whole team can be lifted.

Attraction and Retention of Talent

Now that the four principles of a winning team are in place, a CPO needs to find ways of successfully attracting and retaining some highly talented individuals to the team. A recent Efficio survey of Procurement business leaders revealed that training and development is one of the surest ways to do this (*The Human Factor*, Sept 2019). And it's easy to see the logic in this. Top talent is invariably ambitious and understands that to progress it needs ample opportunity to learn and grow.

In some cases, Procurement functions, if they offer any training at all to their team members, will stick to what is seen as the core Procurement syllabus of negotiation and perhaps some other technical Procurement training, such as contracting. Some companies go further and sponsor their employees to pursue Procurement qualifications, such as CIPS (Chartered Institute of Procurement &

Supply). There is no doubt that courses like these can be beneficial and, in the case of CIPS, it is a qualification that is recognized across the industry. This does help some companies to attract people to come and work in their Procurement function. But are these the right people?

There are drawbacks to this approach. The first is that too strong a focus on technical skills in Procurement misses what really makes a high-performing Procurement person. As we have laid out in this chapter, broader analytical and commercial skills are much more important, as is having the right soft skills to build trust and then influence stakeholders. There is little focus on these skills in technical Procurement courses.

The second drawback of this approach is that it is one-size-fits-all. Some CPOs will view training as a box that needs ticking and for ease will send sections of the team on certain courses, with no expectation for further learning. But this is not nearly as effective as allowing tailored learning for individuals in the team based on their individual needs, which are unlikely to be the same. This is much easier to do today than it was 20 years ago when training nearly always had to be classroom-based.

Today, we live in an era of cheap information. You can literally learn about anything online these days, often for free. Viewed through this lens, there really is no reason why individuals in the Procurement team should not be encouraged—or freed up, depending on how you look at it—to design their own training syllabus and take their learning into their own hands. Clearly the environment for this needs to be set up by the CPO, who must embed a culture of self-learning. This means encouraging and supporting self-awareness of training needs—or, even better, ambitions—and then checking in with the employee, at least during the performance review cycle, to see what sources of knowledge they have been able to find to facilitate that.

Some good examples of learning that can be pursued in this way that falls outside of traditional Procurement training would be data visualization, influencing skills, even sales skills. The point, however, is that they should cover whatever it is the individual wants to learn to help them be better at their role and therefore make a more valuable contribution to the company.

Of course, self-learning and self-motivation can't be completely relied upon to take the place of a more standard approach to training everyone on the team on a perceived common skills gap. However, even here there are improvements to be had in how training in Procurement is traditionally delivered. E-learning has been around for a long while, but still some Procurement functions have not taken the plunge. By giving their employees more flexibility in terms of when and how they consume training, whether through e-learning or even a mobile device, the impact of the training is likely to be higher.

The other, more important, side to the learning equation is "learning by doing." And this is particularly important in Procurement, where the actual technical skills are straightforward and not even a major prerequisite for success. You can focus solely on training and absorbing concepts but, unless you spend your time trying new things out in real life, you will only progress so far. This has often been a weakness of traditional Procurement functions with static roles. You do the same role day in, day out, and there is little opportunity to try something different or get exposed to new things. And it's not very attractive to an ambitious, highly talented person and not likely to be enough to retain them either.

As we have already discussed, when building a winning team, a key principle that a CPO needs to adhere to is keeping that team versatile and employing people in project roles, moving them from one project to the next as priorities and demand change. Not only does this give the Procurement team the agility it needs, but it also gives the highly talented people in Procurement the constant source of learning opportunities that they often demand. Suddenly Procurement goes from being a job that is similar for 10 years to a career that offers new experiences and variety every few months!

In fact, the CPO should go further than this and not be afraid to allow his or her best people to leave Procurement to go and work in other functions within the business. By doing this, it opens up Procurement as a function for many people who would never have dared go near it, thinking that once they were in Procurement, they were trapped unless they moved to a different company.

The highest-performing Procurement organizations make a point of helping their best people to leave to go elsewhere in the company because, on many occasions, the people come back more rounded. Highly talented individuals are also happy to be rotated into Procurement, knowing it's not a dead end.

Critically, the skills we have spoken about in this chapter that make successful Procurement people are transferable, such that they can be successful in most functions. Procurement just needs to make sure it is one of the seats on the merry-go-round for talented individuals who want a successful career in a company.

Being Bold When Hiring

As we've discussed, when it comes to recruitment, Procurement experience is often sought after in candidates. The reason is clear: it seems like the least risky strategy. If someone has 10 years of Procurement experience, then surely they will do well in a winning Procurement team. No one could possibly get in trouble if it doesn't work out, given they are tried and tested in a Procurement function.

Given what we have said in this chapter about successful Procurement people, however, Procurement experience should be a nice to have, at best. The technical side of Procurement is not rocket science, and the concepts can be learned quickly by bright people. By narrowing your search for people to build that winning team to those who have spent significant time in Procurement, you are eliminating huge swaths of the brightest, most high potential candidates. The remaining pool without doubt has some excellent people in it but not enough to go around!

In our view, a company would do better to hire bright, motivated people irrespective of any previous Procurement experience—for example, from Sales or even graduates straight from university—because it will be easier to find candidates with the skills to ensure the Procurement team is a winning one. It is interesting to note that the consulting houses hire according to this model. They generally take people from good universities, with a rounded personality and often a science-related degree, but no Procurement experience. They teach them the technical Procurement concepts very quickly, and they often achieve excellent results with their clients. They can help their clients achieve these results because generally these candidates are motivated, they want to learn, they have excellent analytical and commercial skills, and they relate well to their clients and the people with whom they need to work.

Of course, this model is not necessarily one-to-one transferable to industry, but by being bold and hiring for tomorrow's winning team rather than the traditional Procurement skillset, CPOs will have a much greater chance of pleasing internal customers, getting traction in the business, and raising the Procurement profile. In doing so, Procurement becomes an attractive function in which to work and breaks the low visibility cycle that has plagued it for so long.

5

OPERATING MODEL: Making It Work in Practice

Documenting the Future Model

Throughout this book we talk about the elements that allow companies to profit from Procurement. And we believe there is significant scope for this—whether that is through setting the right ambition, getting the right team in place, understanding how to execute high quality Strategic Sourcing, measuring savings, making the right technology decisions, and more. Yet there is one element that is fundamental to all these others. It is the foundation upon which all the others depend. Without this element, you wouldn't be able to achieve your ambition, and you wouldn't get much value from your technology. Your team could not reach its potential, and you certainly would struggle to execute Strategic Sourcing well to continue to bring ever more value to your company.

That element is an operating model, and it is the thing that brings and then holds everything together. If you work in a Procurement function, especially a larger one, then it's quite possible you will have documented your operating model. If so, it was probably the result of a deliberate workstream to improve it from a previous state. Your operating model will describe how your people work and what they should do.

61

It describes how they are organized. And it describes how these people interact with technology, data, and processes.

So far, so standard. This is surely not news to anyone. But this is precisely the problem some organizations have with their documented Procurement operating model. It describes how they *should* work but not how they *actually* work.

Before we discuss what is perhaps the hardest part of the operating model, which is how to make the transition from the current to the desired ways of working, we should first talk briefly about the steps behind defining a to-be model. We expect most readers will be familiar with this, but it's worth recapping.

Having a vision is the first step. As we discussed in the second chapter on "Ambition," this needs to be aligned to the strategy of the business. What are the goals, objectives, and risks of the business and how does the supply chain, and Procurement specifically, contribute to those—positively or negatively? With this as the context, what is the mission of Procurement?

Cost optimization will likely be a key part, as we have discussed elsewhere in the book, but not necessarily the only part. This mission is then ready to be translated into your vision statement for the Procurement function.

Good vision statements are clear and easy to understand for the uninitiated. Free from jargon, they succinctly articulate Procurement's desired and realistic contribution to the business, which aligns perfectly with the business's overall strategy. This last point is crucial because it means there should be no conflict with other functions when setting out to achieve the vision.

Next, CPOs focus on how this vision breaks down across the elements of the Procurement function. There are many models out there that describe the different elements of the Procurement function, but they can almost always be summarized as people, data and processes, and technology. An example of a framework for this that we have seen many companies use in the past is as follows: Strategy and Organization; Demand and Stakeholder Management; Sourcing Process; Settlement Process; Supplier Management; Policies, Controls, and Compliance; Technology and Data; and People Skills and Incentives (**see Figure 5.1**).

Elements of a Procurement Function

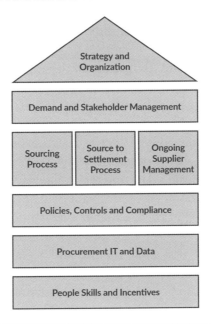

Figure 5.1 **Elements of a Procurement Function**

For a more in-depth look at how this type of exercise can be used as part of planning the roadmap for your transformation, see Chapter 13: Roadmap.

At this point CPOs will, correctly, ask themselves the following sorts of questions: What is the current status of my function against each of these dimensions, and what are the one-, two- and three-year goals for each based on my vision statement? What objectives does that create for my function in the short-, medium- and long-term? Based on where I am today, what are the gaps and change requirements? How can these be organized into workstreams and sub-initiatives that form an overall plan?

By answering these questions, gaps are identified between the as-is and to-be, and recommendations are deduced. For example, perhaps the team needs to mirror the structure of the business to better serve it, or the team needs some additional skills that can be obtained through training or other learning opportunities. Sometimes a new Procurement policy is necessary with some technology enablement. Finally, the new operating model is sketched out which includes organigrams, roles and responsibility maps (RACI diagrams), skills profiles, and new processes.

It's important to note that, while understanding what the best in the industry are doing in these dimensions is useful as you work to sketch out this to-be model, you need to understand the dimensions on which you want to focus. Understand what Procurement is going to excel at in this business, based on the business priorities and relative strength and weaknesses of other functions, and pick two to three elements at most. Perhaps it's data and technology. Or perhaps it's market expertise. That does not mean you are not going to be good at other elements but functions that try to excel at everything sometimes struggle to excel at anything.

Once you've got this to-be picture and a plan to get there from your current state, it's important to socialize it and test it with other key departments to see how their vision, plan, and objectives align or conflict with yours, tweaking if necessary. The most important thing about a to-be model is that it supports the overall corporate strategy and that of peer functions.

The Center-Led Approach

The foundational layer

One of the key questions you will need to answer when designing and documenting your model is how much to centralize your Procurement function. This is the foundational layer. While a purely centralized function is suitable for some organizations, and many organizations have decentralized functions following years of acquisition and lack of integration across companies, a more balanced center-led function has become the most common practice in recent years for companies wanting to get ahead. And this is true not only of the Procurement function. Center-led functions for HR, IT, and other functions that have traditionally played a supporting role in business, have become common.

In the center-led model, each of the dimensions of the framework we have just touched on are centralized (which means ways of working defined by the center), but there is an element of freedom at a local level, be it geographic or business unit, to apply those standards and practices. For example, in the center-led function the sourcing and supplier management processes become standardized but may contain additional steps that can be applied locally.

The benefits of the center-led model are numerous. Firstly, it allows a company to properly leverage its spend. By centralizing demand, it is able to leverage spend and take advantage of economies of scale. It also enables the leveraging of talent across the business. With a central oversight of people in the organization sitting both centrally and locally, ensuring the right skills exist in the right places and sharing knowledge between otherwise disparate resources is much easier.

Centralized processes ensure consistency of approach and a familiar customer experience each time someone from the business interacts with Procurement. This is especially important in elevating the Procurement function and building credibility with stakeholders. And with centralized systems, there is a common language and one version of the truth—particularly in relation to spend, contract, and supplier performance data. Without this one version of the truth and solid master data that underpins it, your ability to be a reliable provider of insight that can drive decision making is severely limited, as we discuss in more detail in Chapter 10: Technology.

But by allowing a level of freedom to local geographies and business units to interpret and apply some of these standards to suit their needs, you retain some agility which is required to keep those geographies and business units operating effectively. Too much dictating from the center can be inappropriate.

Which leads us on to how you go about grounding the above theory in reality to make the model work. This is where the art really lies, in knowing how much to centralize to drive economies of scale and optimize ways of working while maintaining flexibility to accommodate local requirements and nuances. There are a number of things to consider.

Firstly, you should look at how the other functions are set up. Remember we spoke about HR and IT earlier in the chapter?

Well, are they center-led? Perhaps they are completely decentralized. Knowing how they are set up is important because there might be a reason why that is so, and it's quite possible that could be what works best in the company. Understanding the reasons behind their current setup will be useful to you in deciding what to do with your Procurement function.

Secondly, are you master of your Procurement universe? Many CPOs are not. Maybe IT has its own Procurement and vendor management team. Perhaps there are global process owners for some of your Procurement processes who don't even sit in Procurement. Or maybe Marketing has refused to engage with Procurement for the last few years. Depending on the answers to some of these questions, you will need to pick your battles when deciding how much to control and then centralize each element. It's also important to note at this point the readiness of your company to move to the model you want. Maybe you can identify the end state, but if the company is not ready for that end state then considering a phased approach is best.

And finally, what are the structures of the supply markets and commonality of business needs? Where regional or global supply bases are mature and can serve approximately 80% of business requirements, then the opportunity exists to leverage the full category spend in a more efficient manner by directing category strategies and supplier selection centrally. Similarly, if business needs are common, or can be harmonized, this provides the opportunity to drive efficiency and create a larger common volume to be leveraged.

So, given this, what are the implications for the organization design? Effective global Procurement always needs an element of central leadership as we have discussed so far to shape the direction and drive the program. Two models are common. A "thin" model with a small central leadership function directing and coordinating policy, strategy, and direction—but with the actual sourcing activity led by local teams on a delegated basis, with lead-buyers appointed in the regions—is usually the one with the largest spend concentration.

This is a commonly adopted model for confederated global businesses, but getting it right is not easy, as a common risk is the delegated regional category lead not having the effective remit or incentive to deliver value for business outside their own region. It is therefore common in this model to change reporting lines for these staff into the central CPO to help coordinate and drive action.

The second is a "thick" model, more common in companies with higher correlations of global oligopoly supply markets and very similar business needs. In this model, certain spend categories are designated as global, and the full category management accountability sits with a central team, managing specific categories on behalf of regional business units. This model is common in global Manufacturing and fast-moving consumer goods (FMCG) companies, and can drive significant efficiency as well as provide stronger coordination in supply base investment, innovation, and product development.

The category layer

Once you have decided on the extent to which to centralize your function, it is important to decide how you are going to set up your major spend categories. And just because you have a centralized function, it doesn't mean that central Procurement is going to manage all of your spend categories. For some categories that might be appropriate; but for others you might, for example, have a central strategy but allow the local geographies and business units to apply it locally. Or you might have categories that will be set up in a more decentralized manner and are managed by the business.

One of the most effective approaches we have seen to getting to the right model for each category is to set up a category council that consists of all the key people (for example, budget holders, Engineering, Procurement, end users, and divisional managers, or their equivalents) deciding on the overall strategy, supplier roster, and supplier management program, including defined roles and responsibilities in a fully integrated and aligned way.

For an indirect category it is likely that Procurement will be in the lead with input from the rest, but for other categories Procurement has a more supporting role and embeds itself in the relevant operations function with a dotted reporting line from the function to Procurement. This way, the Procurement model provides the advantages of centralization and standardization, while safeguarding the specific requirement of category characteristics by applying a flexible, integrated and custom-built way of working with business partners.

Another organizational aspect to consider, when setting up categories of spend, is how to staff them. For many years, there was a trend to put in place a category manager model, where it was the category manager's responsibility to address the category spend only—which often meant working across many different stakeholders who shared that category spend.

More recently, organizations have deployed a business partnering model where the Procurement organization mirrors the business functions, essentially allowing Procurement to better man-mark its internal customers. This latter model involves having a roving pool of sourcing managers beneath these business partners that harness the synergies from the different business areas. We talk more about our recommendations in this area in Chapter 4: People.

Ultimately though, these are all just org charts. What's more important is how it actually works.

Shifting from Reactive to Proactive

Building your to-be model and working out how to organize yourself globally is all well and good. But at this point it is vital not to fall into the trap of expecting a Procurement organization to make a huge leap from as-is to to-be almost overnight, because this won't happen. Not only is it far too much change at once, but it assumes people can start working on very different activities almost immediately, with a different focus, without finding a solution for all the stuff they are busy with today, however non-value adding that stuff may be.

No new org chart on a PowerPoint document by itself has changed how people work. Done only in this way, as it sometimes is, the new documented Procurement operating model will lie in a cupboard and gather dust. And people will carry on largely as before. The biggest and most common mistake people make is not paying any attention to the next step, which is how to operationalize your new model. How are you going to get to where you've identified that you need to go? The answer is that you need to organically grow into your to-be model from where you are today.

One big reason the transition to to-be can be so hard is that Procurement can sometimes be a very reactive function. And when it creates a new model to work to, the implementation of that model involves Procurement doing a lot of things differently. But to do things differently it needs to have the time and space to be proactive, otherwise it won't be able to stop reacting to the same less value-adding activity that keeps coming from the business in the as-is model.

The business is not going to suddenly start treating Procurement differently on its own. This less value-adding activity could be new supplier requests from the business, urgent contract renewals, operational supplier management (part A has not arrived in warehouse B from supplier C—call Procurement pronto!), being brought into a supplier negotiation at the eleventh hour when it's almost impossible to affect the outcome, and a whole host of other activities. I'm sure at this point any seasoned CPO could come up with a list of 20 or more reactive activities his or her function has got stuck doing in the past.

Just how reactive is Procurement in general today? Well, we have seen studies across a number of industries and sectors that revealed Procurement self-scored that approximately 30% of its work was proactive and strategic versus 70% reactive and minimally value-adding. But if you scratch beneath the surface the true picture is likely to be a lot worse. This is, in fact, the best-case scenario since it was based on the number of strategic roles versus operational roles that exist in Procurement today, amongst those surveyed, and assumes that everyone in an operational role is reacting to business demands and that everyone in strategic roles is being proactive and strategic, all of the time.

The first assumption is fair, the second less so. How many strategic Procurement managers in your business can say they never get dragged into reactive, operational-type work? Or work where no particular skill was required? How many can say it doesn't even happen 50% of the time? Not many, I'd guess!

I was speaking to a client recently, discussing this exact point. He has five strategic Procurement managers in his team that he described as all doing strategic activity 100% of the time. But it turns out that all of them do contract renewals as part of their roles.

And some of these renewals are entering the third or fourth renewal in a mature relationship where value is harder to come by at the renewal stage. It was actually someone in his team who piped up during our conversation with this point! This type of contract renewal is not really that strategic at all.

The true average percentage across industries is likely to be 10–20% of Procurement's time spent doing proactive, strategic activity today—activity it wants to do in order to change its operating model and significantly increase value proposition to the company and then maintain it. And that's not a lot of time!

Just to be clear, being proactive is not just a nice-to-have to help Procurement feel good about itself. It is absolutely critical to the survival of the function itself! This is because sooner or later this reactive and lower value-adding activity will be automated or done elsewhere in the business if Procurement is perceived as a bottleneck, which it can sometimes be. Procurement cannot afford to wait for this to happen. It needs to orchestrate the change and reposition itself before this is something that happens to Procurement. See Chapter 10: Technology, for how we think Procurement must learn from the plight of high street real estate agents in this regard!

Given this prognosis, how much activity that a Procurement function does should be proactive and strategic? Well, even if we assume that we are around the 15–20% mark today, we should aspire to 100%. But to get there requires you to take your function on a journey to its new to-be operating model. Below are the necessary steps.

Organic Growth to a Proactive Focus

Step 1: Visibility of work

Once your to-be model is designed, agreed, and signed-off, the first critical step is to get visibility of the work of your current team. Do you really know how each of them spends their day? Even the best CPOs might not at a granular level. Yes, Jessica might be running three strategic projects, but does she only spend her time doing that? Or are there other activities that keep her from focusing on what you'd like her to do? And the six tenders that Dermot has on the go—why are they taking so long? Is all that activity really strategic? Or is he spending large swaths of his time dealing with ad hoc requests from the business to contract suppliers with whom they have already negotiated?

A time study of your team is a valuable approach to understanding, at a granular level, what your team spends its time doing. By asking them to log their activities at frequent time intervals over a period you can aggregate the data and categorize it by activity type.

With this analysis—which is likely to surprise you—you can identify the work they are doing that you would like them to do (which helps move you towards your to-be model) and that which you would prefer they didn't. The latter being all the ad hoc and less value-adding work, or work you didn't even know about.

You will also be able to get a picture of the true scope of your function, which has probably not been visible to anyone in the business until now—at least not outside of Procurement. Of course, there will be a documented scope somewhere, but that is worth little if the reality is different.

I once worked with a Procurement function in which the consensus amongst people outside the function was that the vast majority of time was spent doing contract renewals and negotiating deals with some of the largest strategic vendors. But, while they did indeed do these things, a time study revealed some of the supposed key workers spent less than 20% of their time on these tasks and the remainder of their time: enforcing the company's mobile device and travel policies, maintaining an insurance tracker for the business and its plethora of business units to ensure each had the right cover, maintaining a large central register of office locations across the group for the many buildings it owned and leased, chasing the business for contracts to ensure compliance to regulation, coordinating the onboarding of suppliers with the business to ensure they met the relevant information security requirements, and chasing current and former suppliers to check adherence to the new General Data Protection Regulation that had just been brought in.

This sort of scope is more obviously less value-adding. But going back to our earlier example, on something like contract renewals, even part of supposedly strategic work can itself be less value-adding. Particularly if poor data and systems exist that call for hours of manual data manipulation.

No one is saying that you can just give up this sort of less valuable scope right away, but it is important to know your starting point accurately before piling more and different scope onto an already stretched team to get to a new to-be model. That is how the operating model initiative will fail.

The granular time study can be a one-off exercise, but another key outcome of this Step 1 on creating visibility of work is a dynamic view of what people are working on, at a slightly higher level, refreshed regularly. What initiatives are they working on? What is the expected benefit of those initiatives, and what are the expected timelines? You want to be able to review this regularly, as things change. Because without that, you can't take the next step.

Step 2: Start prioritizing

And that next step is prioritization. Really effective prioritization. To illustrate this, let's assume your Procurement team is maxed out doing unproductive work. Even if it is not, and it does some strategic tasks already, this methodology will still help you to reduce less value-adding work irrespective of how much is being done today by your team. Such work represents an opportunity to focus on more strategic and proactive Procurement activity that will help you progress to your to-be model.

To prioritize effectively, you need to ask probing questions of the current team and to get under the skin of what they are doing and why they are doing it. This requires a critical and questioning mindset towards current work mix. The types of questions to ask are:

- Are we triaging new requests effectively?
- Is the Procurement team working outside its remit and expectation?
- Can we enable the business to do more themselves?
- Are other teams a bottleneck (maybe Legal?)?
- Are we constantly reinventing the wheel?
- Are we using support teams effectively, if they exist?

With visibility of work created in Step 1, you can begin answering these questions.

And with these answers you can start to make some small tweaks to how things work and deploy some enablers. These enablers should help to provide some of the solutions to the issues thrown up by answering the previous questions.

Enablers can come in many forms: knowledge injection, specific skills, potentially even a new tool to automate or facilitate a task, if done correctly. For example, maybe we found in Step 1 that analysis of supplier bids saps time from the team due to manual reconciliation of bid sheets and then needing to build and run formulae to calculate possible supplier award scenarios. If that is the case, one enabler could be to create a standard approach to this analysis and build a template with a level of automation. Or let's suppose that three sourcing initiatives don't seem to be moving past the strategy phase because the business can't decide what commercial model it wants, creating a huge drag on three people's time in the team. We could buy in some external expertise to help run through options with the business in a day-long workshop to unblock this impasse.

If your team is maxed out—which it almost certainly will be whatever it is doing—then it's entirely possible you might need to find a short-term solution outside of your immediate team to do the prioritization task … a person able to find answers to the critical questions we discussed earlier. This is not a long- or even medium-term solution.

The principle should be build, transfer, operate; and then those tasks should be conducted within your own team as soon as possible once the first bit of time is freed up for it. Enablers should also be brought into your current team where possible but, in reality, there is likely to be a mix of internal and external enablers. For example, you may choose to outsource market research to support your sourcing strategies rather than have your team all try to do market research themselves in different ways. Or you might engage with an expert network that gives you access to category insight that allows you to unblock category strategies in the way we described earlier.

Figure 5.2 illustrates this process. And we have just spoken about moving from Phase 1 to Phase 2.

Strategic Sourcing Governance

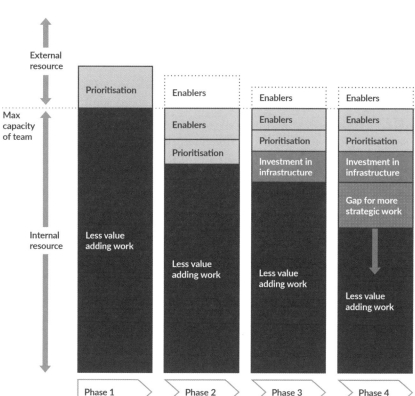

Figure 5.2   Strategic Sourcing Governance

The aim of this prioritization step is to get to Phase 4, which is where a gap in your team's capacity starts to appear—a gap that you can fill with new, more strategic activity and help you get to your to-be operating model!

But before we move to that, how to get from Phase 2 to Phase 3? The answer is, as soon as your inhouse Project Management Office (PMO) and enablers help you to free up capacity in your team, you should resist filling it with strategic activity straightaway. If you do, then that will be the limit of the strategic activity you will be able to manage going forward. Better is to use that freed up time to find ways of freeing up yet more time. We are calling this an investment in infrastructure, but what does this mean?

Well, it's similar to how we got from Phase 1 to Phase 2, but these are probably the first workstreams on your to-be implementation plan. For example, building a library of templates for people to help them do Strategic Sourcing more effectively in the future or building a knowledge management capability to ensure there is less reinvention of the wheel. When someone has strategically sourced the Chemicals category, how do we ensure that the prices, the suppliers, the strategies, and tender documents are all easily accessible and useable next time? By investing in this infrastructure, you are going to make further capacity gains going forward as you're helping your team be more effective.

Once we're at Phase 3, we will start to see those capacity gains grow, and we'll get to Phase 4. How we use that gap is now critical. And we need to be realistic here as well. If we have the same team with the same skills as before, then parts of the team might get exposed with the new demands for more strategic work. This is where the people part of your operating model comes in, and we discuss that in detail in Chapter 4: People. Ensuring you have the skills in your team to handle and excel at the new type of work you want it to do is, of course, just as critical as freeing up your team to do it.

Step 3: Build and maintain a hopper of opportunities

To ensure we use the extra capacity productively, we need to know what we are going to do with it. This means building a hopper of opportunities—a hopper of strategic activity for which there is a strong value proposition. These opportunities can vary in nature. They may be Strategic Sourcing opportunities; they may be opportunities for better supplier management. Perhaps opportunities for further bettering the infrastructure that exists to make the Procurement function yet more efficient and its people yet more effective. But before getting onto the hopper, let's clarify what is happening to the less value-adding work in this methodology.

Some of this less valuable work disappears, due to people being able to work more effectively through the enablers of technology, knowledge management, and better prioritization, as we have described here. But as Procurement starts to move towards its new model, it will also be able to better segment its workforce into those who do strategic work and those who don't. The diagram and this methodology become important for the team that is left doing the strategic work, and the less value-adding work can be passed to a more dedicated administrative sub-team or, in other cases, pushed back to the business.

Back to the hopper. The hopper is critical because it also allows Procurement to be flexible and agile—and especially in the face of a crisis such as COVID-19. With time freed up and a portfolio of strategic tasks ready to deploy that are proactive, Procurement can decide what it needs to work on to best serve the business. But, critically, with this visibility it also understands the opportunity cost of not doing certain activities.

When I was working with a UK-based client in the Leisure and Tourism industry in 2020, we had been able to transform its operating model during the previous 18 months to focus on more value-adding and strategic tasks, such as getting more value from critical suppliers and reducing supply chain risk. We were also doing a number of Strategic Sourcing activities. When the COVID-19 crisis hit, the business was impacted severely. All its locations had to close for months, due to government restrictions on staying away from home, and some of the longer sourcing activities the company had been doing were no longer a priority. What was important now was cash preservation. With no revenue to speak of for the foreseeable future, strategically sourcing consumer type categories was a complete irrelevance.

But, because there was a hopper of opportunities, it was able to delve into that during a time of crisis and act quickly in the interests of the company. Pushing out supplier payment terms without putting those businesses in danger became a number one priority. But, because we had an opportunity long-list, some pre-crisis activities continued. In short, the team was able to quickly pivot to the most value-adding portfolio of initiatives for the time because it had a holistic view of all opportunities and benefits.

Isn't This Just Agile?

Well, isn't it? I suppose the answer is, "Yes." The moral of this chapter is not to simply identify where you are and where you want to go and document then the entire, long path to get there. That is the classic approach that can end in Procurement functions never really changing what they do, because you can't possibly predict that path.

If you want to ensure you successfully achieve a new Procurement operating model, you need to identify where you are and where you want to go, but then start to feel your way there, organically. You need to be comfortable stepping out on your journey to the to-be model, able to see the destination but not the whole path. If we jump back to Step 2 of this chapter's three-step methodology, the key is not to ask your people to start "doing more Strategic Sourcing" or "executing better supplier relationship management" to achieve a new operating model, but rather to figure out how to give them the time to do these new activities. Work together to figure out the path.

An absolutely key element of agile in Procurement is having the flexibility to chop and change what you are working on. And that is why a fundamental principle of designing a new Procurement operating model is to ensure you have a team that can be versatile, just like we discussed in Chapter 4: People. Any new, to-be model needs to avoid fixed roles, if at all possible—which is to say, a role in which the person only focuses on one type of activity or category. That is a thing of the past. An agile, and therefore successful, Procurement function needs people who can work across activities—people who can move from one opportunity in the hopper to the other as the business need dictates. That is how you will achieve your to-be model.

6

CROSS-FUNCTIONAL CHANGE: Repositioning the Function as a True Partner

This chapter is somewhat shorter than the other chapters in this book. Cross-functional change management is a key theme that runs through all the chapters of this book, so in order to avoid excessive repetition, we've kept this one relatively short and to the point.

Why Is Cross-Functional Change Management Important?

Procurement is very much seen as a profession / a function of experts that do a discrete thing. The problem is, as soon as you view it that way, you limit its potential by casting it as separate from the other functions.

Procurement's very existence is cross-functional by nature—it only exists in order to help those functions procure their supplies. And, of course, while Procurement can influence, in most companies, 50% to 80% of the cost base, it doesn't actually "own" any of this spend and is not ultimately in charge. That makes life difficult ... it means that Procurement can't do its job out of a position of authority, but it must use sophisticated influencing skills to work effectively with other functions.

As discussed in Chapter 1: Introduction, in many companies the budget-holders effectively do their own Procurement ... with Procurement just coming in at the end to finalize contracts and, at best, negotiate an extra discount at the eleventh hour. The problem is that the budget-holders don't necessarily have the skill, or the objective, of optimizing the cost of what they buy ... they care far more about reliability and other factors. They do care about cost, but the task of optimizing it is secondary to the other factors, and often they just don't know how to go about it. Of course, their primary incentive often lies elsewhere—keeping the line running, keeping the network secure ... which are higher-order objectives compared to optimizing the cost of a spare part or component.

But that's exactly why there is a need for a commercial force—one that is incentivized to optimize the total cost of ownership and to work alongside budget-holders to represent the commercial perspective. And it makes sense to have a function like Procurement, one that is expert at facilitating a Procurement process that seeks a balance between capability and cost, an approach that packages up the budget-holder's needs and then generates attractive commercial options from the supply market. But clearly, it's no easy task ... and the ability to work effectively with the other functions is absolutely critical for success.

Procurement Often Lacks the Required Skills and Mindset

Procurement often doesn't know *how* to work collaboratively and cross-functionally with budget-holders. Having the ability to influence and persuade others is a rare skillset, especially when it comes to influencing senior management. But these skills are critical for Procurement success, as is the right *mindset*.

As we saw in Chapter 1: Introduction, Procurement functions sometimes don't help themselves, by adopting a policeman / compliance-type role ("It *has* to go through Procurement!") ... which is of course highly off-putting to the other functions. Insistence on process ("We have to get three quotes; this is how Procurement does it.") is also very unhelpful in getting others on your side!

To be fair, and as already said, it's not an easy ask to be tasked with working collaboratively with other parts of the business, who may not welcome you being involved on their turf in the first place. But that doesn't matter ... working effectively cross-functionally is a skill that Procurement desperately needs to have.

How Do We Do It Effectively?

So, what's the answer? How do we do it? How do you work effectively cross-functionally in an influencing capacity? We suggest seven success factors:

1. You need to execute well and have good deliverables.
2. You need to engage formally and meaningfully at all levels.
3. You need to use effective stakeholder engagement skills.
4. You need to exhibit a service mindset.
5. You need to position yourself internally as a proactive dealmaker.
6. You need to share credit, and help rather than take away.
7. You need air cover.

Let's briefly examine each in turn. You will recognize these points by now, so we'll try to be brief.

1) You need to execute well and have good deliverables

In Procurement, you're providing a service by sourcing the budget-holder's spend on his or her behalf; therefore, you need to earn your right to be in the room. If you don't add value, why are you there? the budget-holder rightly asks. On a human level, what it boils down to is that the budget-holder is going to assess your capability: "Well then show me, let's see what you've got." And at this point, you need to impress. You need to command respect from the representative of the other function, so that they can see that you're a high-caliber, value-adding resource.

So, how do you impress? Well, you do it in a number of ways, but in business, you do it first and foremost by executing well (for example, organizing structured and effective supplier review meetings, following up on all actions, and more).

Next, you earn respect through your "deliverables." Granted, this is consulting speak ... but along the category management journey, there are a number of deliverables—spend analysis, category baseline, supply market analysis, sourcing strategy, RFI document, supplier long-list, RFP document, RFP bids analysis output, negotiation packs, supplier management plans. These are what you deliver: in many ways, they are your product, and their quality speaks volumes about you. Simple things: a half-assed supplier long-list suggests that you're not great at your job; an excellent supplier long-list suggests that you're very good at it. Simple as that.

So, do make sure your team's deliverables are of the highest-possible quality. Anything that goes in front of a stakeholder needs to be buttoned up, accurate, crisp, and clear. And no typos!

2) You need to engage formally and meaningfully at all levels

Again, we've talked about this at length throughout the book. It sounds obvious, but this is where buyers and category managers often just don't have enough time; and you need to put the time in, you need to listen and get to know your stakeholders and their objectives, their issues, what keeps them awake at night. If you don't have the time, you need to make it! See Chapter 5: Operating Model, for suggestions on how to rebalance the Procurement team's activities. And when you do effect a change in their time allocation, make sure there's plenty of time for stakeholders.

You also need to engage *formally*: *not* through corridor chats, but through structured meetings and powerful workshops where things are decided; for example, a negotiations strategy workshop, a supplier shortlisting workshop, a specification harmonization workshop. These mechanisms get everyone in the room involved and enable you to drive to decisions—as long as these workshops are well-prepared and executed.

The *quality* of the engagement is also important, and quality engagement is what moves things forward. It's when you have proper, intelligent, meaningful dialogue that things get resolved and the right outcome for all parties concerned is chosen.

When you do engage, of course, you don't just talk. You need to make sure you *align*; you need to make sure everyone is in agreement. This takes some effort, but it's effort well spent. So, before that big Steering Committee meeting, you need to pre-brief the CEO, the CFO, the COO, the CIO, the Head of the Americas (and in the right order) ... so that they're aligned going into the meeting. You need to be engaging and aligning horizontally (across functions), but also vertically—up and down the organization chart in terms of seniority.

And let's not forget the suppliers. The more you've talked to all of them, the more credible you are. Even better if you spend a bit of time on the shop floor, like the consultant with whom I recently spent a full week in an auto repair body shop before sourcing the category for an insurer. His credibility went through the roof, because he'd invested time in understanding how things work bottom up—from a supplier's perspective *and* from a shop floor perspective.

We've talked at length elsewhere about how to structure a formal program, and how the associated formal governance structure facilitates formal cross-functional representation at all levels—both in the sourcing / execution teams and in the Executive Steering Committee. Structuring work in a formal program naturally fosters a degree of cross-functionality and should be the modus operandi wherever possible.

3) You need to use effective stakeholder engagement skills

This is not about using some fancy change management tool to map your stakeholders on a three-dimensional matrix. This is about the fundamental change management skills of listening, empathy, influencing, persuasion ... the soft skills that will win your stakeholders over.

In my 27-year Procurement consulting career, poor stakeholder engagement skills are by far the biggest deficit we see in Procurement functions. Their buyers often don't know how to influence, let alone persuade people. And you can see that because of this, they can't break through to the stakeholder, and so they don't move forward. It's heart-breaking.

And yet, these soft skills can be learned and acquired to a very significant degree: presentation skills, influencing skills, Neuro-linguistic proramming (NLP)—there are plenty of training programs out there. Procurement training is traditionally too focused on the hard skills of negotiating and contracting. But those don't get you in the door!

4) You need to exhibit a service mindset

This, we have also talked about in Chapter 1: Introduction. You are there to serve; it's not your spend, you are a support function. So, don't adopt policeman tactics ... instead, use a mindset of "We are here to serve you, but we *will* try to influence you in the commercially right direction." But don't be a push-over either, which is extremely common in Procurement—buyers afraid to challenge their stakeholders. Service mindset does not mean push-over.

Part of that service mindset is understanding who the ultimate decision maker is, and that is unequivocally the budget-holder. Do *not* try to argue that supplier selection is Procurement's decision. What utter rubbish! What Procurement needs to do is to show a range of fully negotiated commercial options, with pros and cons attached to each; it can highlight the trade-off in cost for going for the higher cost option, but no more.

A lot of being successful cross-functionally is to just act professionally and courteously. Being polite, listening to the other party, showing humility, being their support function that elicits their needs and builds the category strategy around them and their priorities ... these things go a long way.

5) You need to position yourself internally as a proactive dealmaker

As with everything in life, you need to be proactive. Don't wait for the contract to expire and then get called in to muddle through a last-minute extension ... be on the front foot. *Originate* exciting new deals and opportunities, don't simply react.

And don't leave it all to your people; the job of PR is the CPO's job. You need to go sell your function internally, and you need to bring exciting opportunities to the table. And you can only do that if you're proactive, if you're talking to suppliers, talking to peers to compare notes, learning about the latest supply market developments. A dealmaker is forever scouring for that deal, so you need to keep your eyes and ears open and cast a wide net. And then you need to strike and bring the opportunity to the table in a compelling way. The "art of origination" should be part of the cross-functional contract. A high-performing Procurement function *must* be highly proactive.

6) *You need to share credit, and help rather than take away*

If you want to get along with others, don't set yourself up as a competitor for "credit"—that goes for qualitative credit for the effort, but also for who gets "financial credit" for the savings. It's inescapable that there is an overlap when it comes to savings, because Procurement is generating a saving in someone else's budget. Don't let this be a source of conflict; have Finance manage this issue. As we will discuss in Chapter 9: Savings Realization, Finance should position Procurement as the hero, by applying their budget haircut *before* Procurement is deployed.

And another tip from the consultants … they're good at getting buy-in because their ethos is to operate behind the scenes and let the client take all the glory. It works, and it can be applied to Procurement. Procurement facilitates, operates behind the scenes, and lets the budget-holder be the hero … don't worry, you'll get your credit—people know when you've done good work.

7) *You need air cover*

Again, we have discussed this in a number of chapters, but it's worth stressing again. Without appropriate air cover, you will fail. You can't do this job alone, you need the CEO and the CFO as a bare minimum, to root for you all the way.

What does this mean, specifically? It means that they need to give you the remit that you need, and then tell the rest of the organization that you now have that remit. At a recent client, a strengthened Procurement remit was agreed explicitly and in detail with the CFO and with the new Private Equity owners, but it was never communicated to the rest of the organization. Unfortunately, this is common, but it isn't helpful. The organization needs to be told that Procurement is coming!

Next, your sponsors need to remove the roadblocks you encounter that you can't overcome by yourself. Execution is hard, and blockages are constant—the sponsors need to actually help! They are the escalation point for un-sticking cross-functional issues.

In turn, this means that your sponsors have to keep abreast of what you're doing, and at a detailed level. They need to understand the ins and outs of the sourcing strategy, because that's where the conflict will be.

I remember a global insurance brokerage client a few years ago. The whole executive team, the CEO out front, was sitting with us in the conference room during the Procurement Steering Committee and wordsmithing the travel policy with us on the screen. I can tell you that policy really, really got traction, and it's because the sponsors at executive level were personally invested.

Personal investment is good. Beyond the C-Suite, you should ensure that your broader business stakeholders are fully invested. Bring them to executive committee meetings to discuss key Procurement negotiations—that way they're on the hook and will work to make the initiative a success.

Sponsorship needs to be active. "Lip service sponsorship" is not enough.

Specific Functions

All parts of the business have their own characteristics. Finance is a particular function with which Procurement needs to work very closely, and this is addressed in detail in Chapter 9: Savings Realization.

Beyond this, the other "professional" functions, such as Marketing and Legal, need to be engaged intelligently and on their own terms and language. A Marketing Executive is not looking for the cheapest deal when it comes to creative agencies, so stop talking about price!

It's about overall effectiveness and return on Marketing investment, and that's the language you need to use.

The IT function is often a little different to other functions, in that it does much of its own Procurement and supplier management, albeit outside the fold of the Procurement function. IT team members tend to be intelligent people who know what they're doing, and they need to be treated as such. So, to open the door to IT, Procurement needs to articulate how it can help *beyond* what the IT function may already be doing. And it needs to navigate what can often be an ever-shifting, phased roll-out IT strategy, to see where it can best engage and add value.

Finally, the sourcing of Direct Materials requires a good understanding of the downstream processes (for example, Engineering, Manufacturing, Quality), and Procurement needs to adapt to work within the very real constraints of switching costs and the need for supplier certification.

In the end, when it comes to the various functions, the approach is the same, but it pays to speak their language, understand their world, and make sure your ideas fit with their plans.

What Can We Learn from the Consultants?

I'm not talking about "toolkits and techniques" here. These are often what our clients ask for when we talk about change management, and they can be useful. Problem is, in the end, they're often just static observations and plans on a page.

What's more interesting to learn from the consultants is their often-solid execution skills. Good presentation skills, for example, go a hell of a long way towards impressing people, which gets them on board ... good data, good slideware (yes, it matters!), good people engagement skills ... if you bring in consultants, make sure your people watch and learn. The other thing that consultants do well is project management: structure, detail, and discipline. Again, make sure your people pick up some of this good practice along the way.

And again, that service mindset and courteousness—consultants have this in spades, because their clients are external clients that pay their bills rather than internal peers. Procurement can learn from this, as it's a mindset that is helpful in getting things done.

Finally, let's talk about PowerPoint! People who say, "function is more important than form" and deny the need for high quality visuals are missing the point. Your conclusions, your strategy, your personal credibility will be measured by what's on the page. When people sit in a conference room and stare at your slide on the screen, they'll notice all those little errors and nit-pick. So be clear in your visuals, be sure of the message on each page, label the titles and axes of your graphs, show the units, don't show too many decimal places, cite a source, make sure lists of things are Mutually Exclusive and Collectively Exhaustive (MECE) and prioritized, start sentences in a consistent way, don't have typos, *ever* ... and be compelling!

Conclusion

Cross-functional influencing and change is not about change management toolkits, and there is unfortunately no silver bullet for getting other parts of the business to play nicely with you. Ultimately, the answer to change management is to push, push, push relentlessly, while bringing everyone on board along the way.

In the end, of course, you need to deliver an outstanding result—one in which the budget-holder is fully on board and is very happy with his suppliers and the savings ... then you know you've got it right.

7

SUPPLIERS: Engaging Effectively

Procurement as a function sits in a privileged position.

On the one hand, it faces off to its organization—an organization that must successfully deliver products and services to its customers. To do this, the company creates value for its customers through the activities upon which it chooses to focus. Whether that is manufacturing a product, delivering care to patients, serving people food, or whatever else it is that the company does.

But here's the thing … it can only do that with the help of other organizations. Companies generally focus on doing what they do best, and for most other things they work with partners. This is the other half of the Procurement equation. Procurement also faces off to these partners and its suppliers, and it must provide the critical link between them and the business it serves.

Given that there has been a growing trend in recent years for companies to use suppliers to do more for them as the former focuses efforts on being excellent at its core activity, it's hard to think of a more important business juncture at which to sit.

But, for the majority of these suppliers with which a company works, there is not much to write or talk about—certainly not enough to fill a chapter of a book about how to unlock Procurement's profit potential! These are organizations that provide a non-critical product or service … like the stationery supplier to the banking establishment. Sure, the bank needs pens and paper for its employees to enable them to work. But that stationery supplier is never going to give the bank a competitive advantage—neither is the cleaning company that cleans the offices of its customer at the end of every day. Again, these services are necessary to ensure employees can work in a productive, clean and safe environment, but they're never going to result in a competitive advantage.

And this is the key differentiator. Some suppliers *do* have the ability to give their clients a competitive advantage in their market. They provide products and services in a way that directly impacts their client's ability to be better than the competition, whether that is by breaking into new markets or geographies, by increasing the share of an existing market, by improving customer satisfaction, or by reducing risk. With so much riding on these suppliers and the individual relationships a company has with them, it is clear just what an important topic this is for businesses and, by extension, Procurement. Suddenly, one chapter in a Procurement book seems insufficient!

Supplier Management—The Traditional Approach

We've just defined in broad terms what a strategic supplier is. It is an organization that either has the potential to bring its customer a competitive advantage or does so today. They play such an important role that we need to ensure we are thinking about these relationships in the right way. And this is what we will focus this chapter on.

But to help with that thinking, let us first consider the more traditional method of defining your strategic suppliers and conducting supplier management activities. This generally involves you segmenting your suppliers first. You plot them on a matrix with spend volume on one axis and criticality of supply (sometimes referred to as risk) on the other, or some variation of these criteria.

The way suppliers are placed on the matrix is not always scientific and is often impacted by people's existing opinions on how important they think certain suppliers are to them. Nevertheless, this method does provide some logic as to how to segment your suppliers into different categories depending on their relative scores against these criteria.

In this method, those in the top right-hand corner, with the largest spend and most critical risk rating, are your strategic suppliers. In some cases, this is not a bad proxy but unfortunately this exposes the first fundamental flaw in this method, namely actually identifying who your strategic suppliers are!

For a start, it assumes that strategic suppliers are only those suppliers for which the volume of business is high. However, this doesn't always translate into the supplier being able to offer a competitive advantage. Additionally, this picture is only a snapshot in time. It describes the situation today and does not consider the future. What about that small supplier that has the potential to give us a competitive advantage in the future, if only we nurture our relationship with it?

The second fundamental flaw comes from assuming that we can build and maintain truly strategic supplier relationships simply through the introduction of a process, however detailed or fancy. Let's continue explaining the traditional approach so we can see how this flaw arises.

Once this method has (imperfectly) identified your most strategic suppliers, it also categorizes your other suppliers into buckets that according to this methodology are worthy of different approaches to supplier management. Indeed, this is the key output of the matrix; you now have each of your suppliers in 3–4 different buckets that read something like: strategic, medium importance, and everyone else. Depending on the industry, there could be other buckets of suppliers, such as those that need to be tightly managed to ensure compliance with industry regulations. Financial services institutions often have this bucket included.

Now, if getting the most out of supplier relationships was simply about performance and risk management, this is where the approach is useful—at least in terms of providing a common process framework, giving clarity on roles and responsibilities for that framework and maximizing return on the associated activities. By having a logic to understanding the relative importance of suppliers in your supply base, you can determine the level of effort you want to exert to track and manage their performance against certain KPIs and manage risk.

For example, for the least important suppliers the goal should be compliance management only and not to spend any additional effort doing this than is strictly necessary. You will, in all likelihood, decide it is sufficient to do little or no performance measurement or risk mitigation at all or just review the relationship periodically with these suppliers, or by exception. Simply checking that they are providing what they are contracted to provide, for the cost they are contracted for, is enough. And most of this can be automated with some simple processes and technology.

Then we have the suppliers of medium importance, where again you will go through this traditional method to define a process for managing these suppliers. It is likely to include more robust performance management, with perhaps quarterly KPI reporting. Again, this would ideally be enabled by a tool with a process that runs itself, by suppliers inputting data that feeds into easy to interpret dashboards. This will allow the company to take action as required on an as-needed basis. There are likely to be meetings every 6–12 months planned with these suppliers to review performance based on the KPI scores, to mitigate risk, and to explore further opportunities to increase value for money. The goal of the approach to these suppliers should be developing incremental commercial benefits and, again, managing commercial compliance.

Even for both the medium and less important suppliers, however, having a listening approach brings big benefits. Procurement sometimes tends towards imposing its approach and view on these suppliers, as they are viewed as less important. Perhaps, but that doesn't mean they have any less knowledge of their markets and what works well. Treat them with respect, and let them be the experts in their sector.

Finally, the strategic suppliers. And this is where the second fundamental flaw of the traditional approach becomes obvious. Because, while all the words in this traditional approach are right around how we should be approaching this segment of strategic suppliers (mutual revenue generation, innovation partnerships, risk mitigation, joint initiatives), it's almost impossible to get those outcomes from only putting down a process, which is all this traditional approach really does. The mistake people sometimes make is that they try to define the ways of working with strategic suppliers by way of a process and roles and responsibilities, but that will never be enough to deliver the sort of competitive advantage outcomes we are aspiring to here.

For example, I've seen many companies put in place a quarterly business meeting with individual strategic suppliers, with all the top dogs from both sides present. One point on the agenda will be something like innovation. Sounds exciting and forward thinking, but once that meeting starts no one really knows what to talk about or how to approach the meeting. For example, how do you suddenly "innovate" for that section of a meeting that happens once a month or quarter? Innovation is something that needs to happen through a way of working, at all different levels of the relationship, and certainly not just in the middle part of a three-hour quarterly business review with only senior people present.

As a result, these meetings tend, in fact, to resemble the performance and risk management meetings of the medium importance suppliers, which means you end up treating your strategic suppliers simply as medium importance suppliers. You are not going to get a competitive advantage from your strategic suppliers that way!

So, while taking this traditional approach is helpful in documenting and standardizing a company's approach to different types of suppliers, and for defining roles and responsibilities in the company for who should play what role of the process, in our view it only really achieves something for the suppliers that aren't the most strategic. For really getting the most out of strategic suppliers, it has two fundamental flaws: (i) it doesn't properly identify who these strategic suppliers are or should be, and (ii) by treating true strategic supplier management only in terms of a process, it doesn't on its own allow you to build relationships with suppliers that give you a competitive advantage in your market.

Before we move on to talking about alternative ways to think about strategic supplier management, a quick word on roles and responsibilities for this more traditional approach of performance and risk management of suppliers. It's a question we get asked a lot by companies: Who should be responsible for it, Procurement or the business? In our view, Procurement should be the ones defining the approach and framework and driving the right types of behaviors that will allow a company to get the most out of its suppliers. However, Procurement cannot and should not be the place where all vendor owners sit. Many vendor owners should sit in the business. What is important is that there is a balance of commercial and operational approaches for each vendor, and the latter more often than not resides in the business.

The Strategic Supplier—a Competitive Advantage

Anyway, back to understanding what we mean by getting a competitive advantage from a supplier and how that differs from merely putting in a process for treating a big supplier that provides a business-critical service or product. Let us look at an example.

I once worked with a clothing brand that had a leading market position in street wear clothing. For those readers unfamiliar with the clothing industry, it is cut-throat. Fashion and style preferences change rapidly, and customers can and often do move onto the next big style or brand in an instant. Loyalty amongst consumers to clothing brands is thin at best, especially among the demographic most likely to buy street wear.

To give you an idea of how these dynamics drive the industry, brands with the most advanced business models, including the one in our case study, can get a new garment style from concept to shop floor in as little as four weeks. Given all the steps that exist in the process in between—such as design, prototyping, sampling, manufacturing, and delivery—this is a truly remarkable feat. But it's also entirely necessary to have a chance of winning in this market.

So, while this company had the biggest share of streetwear in its geographies, it could not afford to be complacent for a second. With the continuing threat of new market entrants and continual performance improvements of its key competitors, it had to do something new and different every season. As soon as you stand still in that market you go backwards.

Therefore, the company engages its garment manufacturers and raw materials suppliers—the two types of supplier who most matter here—in a way that means it gets an advantage over all other clothing brands that its suppliers also serve. That is not to say these are one-way relationships in which the suppliers don't win either—clearly, they do, otherwise they wouldn't engage in this way—but the focus of this case study is on what a competitive advantage for the client looks like.

To start with, the suppliers consistently put their A-team on all matters for this client. Without fail, their best people are assigned to, for example, each season's hugely important strategy sessions. And this is true of all interactions and management of the relationship at all levels: the suppliers know who their best people are, and they are reserved for the client. This means they deliver their best work for this client.

Secondly, suppliers give the company first and exclusive access to their latest style ideas and fabric innovations. And these innovations come from a deep understanding of what makes their clients clothes popular and successful. They discuss and work through them with the client deciding which ones to choose and which to leave. This way, the client stands a better chance of landing the next big style and growing or cementing its share of the market.

And thirdly, the suppliers give their client total flexibility. They readily and regularly deprioritize Manufacturing capacity for other clients based on demand that comes in from our streetwear brand—particularly useful when you are trying to get something from concept to shop floor in four weeks, as we saw earlier. You can see the competitive advantage this gives the client over other companies also using those suppliers. Of course, other brands will have their own manufacturers and suppliers from which they will demand the same, but without these relationships it would not be possible for these brands to be as successful as they are in their markets.

Make no mistake, these suppliers are completely invested in their client. Their success or failure is intimately tied to that of their client. But they do it because of the benefits that truly strategic supplier management brings to both parties.

So, given what we have just discussed, how many strategic suppliers do you think you have? In our experience, companies often say they have a several strategic suppliers but, when you define it in the terms we have done so far, many end up having fewer than they thought. One CEO with whom we have worked said recently, "We don't have any strategic suppliers." What he meant by that was that his company didn't get anything exceptional out of his suppliers that his competitors didn't get. "And excellent commercials don't count!" he added.

One good test of the answer is to ask the suppliers that you think are your strategic ones how they view working with you. This is where

Procurement can play an important role. It is in a strong position, being more detached from Operations, to step back and have these discussions with suppliers. Operations sometimes think they are the supplier's "best client," but Procurement can ask what the supplier does for its other customers and what barriers exist to providing a competitive advantage. The answers are often revealing!

Shifting the Mindset

In the high-level streetwear example, we have described what it means to get a competitive advantage from suppliers in a particular industry. And, of course, in this example the client has integrated successfully with its supply chain. This type of relationship has huge benefits for suppliers, too. In this example, the suppliers benefit from long term certainty of custom and investment, allowing them to make plans and develop themselves to become a better company. They get access to the plans of their client as early as possible, which enables them to organize themselves to give the best possible service. So, what are the ways of working, the mindsets—beyond the quarterly business meeting we discussed earlier—that give rise to these types of relationships and that give both sides an advantage over their respective competition?

Well, Efficio asked 200+ Procurement leaders from organizations in the U.S. and Europe from different sectors a couple of years ago how they thought strategic supplier partnerships should be characterized (*The Future of Procurement*, October 2018). It's worth noting that this question was framed such that these are really the most strategic suppliers. It's only possible for an organization to have a handful of these at any one time, otherwise the type of relationship we are talking about gets diluted. In any case, the top four responses were 1) transparent commercials, 2) long-term commitments on both sides, 3) early engagement with the supplier, and 4) visibility of upcoming work and business plans.

It's hard to argue with any of these descriptions. Indeed, the streetwear brand example had all of them. Let's take them in turn. Transparent commercials are the one thing buying organizations strive for because it gives certainty that they are getting best value. But they rarely do have this transparency unless they are in a genuine strategic partnership. That is because suppliers will always price in risk wherever they see uncertainty. And uncertainty is pretty much everywhere—especially between two parties. They need to protect themselves in the event something unforeseen happens, unless they completely trust their client. So, really, transparent commercials are just an output of ways of working. If ways of working mean suppliers don't need to price in risk, they won't.

Which leads us on to the remaining three responses, which are all interlinked and are ways of working. A long-term commitment doesn't just mean a long-term contract. It is a mindset that means both parties put aside short-term pain for long-term gain. This is very difficult to do in practice because it requires trust and a shared vision.

I once worked with a telecoms company that had this mindset with one of its strategic technology suppliers. There was a period in which a change in technological requirement meant that the supplier had significant sunk cost in equipment that they were developing. But, because these two organizations worked so closely with each other and had a shared a long-term vision that, when realized, would easily out-weigh even this pain, there was not even a discussion about short-term financial compensation from one side to the other. There was significant trust and understanding that had been built up over years and been reciprocated on each side a few times over by that point. How many organizations can say they have that sort of mindset with their most strategic suppliers?

Next, early engagement with the supplier means exactly what it says. It requires clients to accept that as soon as they start defining a solution without input from their strategic suppliers, or the wider market if appropriate, they are foregoing all the innovation and problem-solving potential that those suppliers could bring to the party as an additional team member.

Some organizations are very good at early supplier engagement, but many are not. Procurement, in particular, has a habit of wanting to define requirements to a detailed and granular level before engaging the market. In some instances that is appropriate, but for goods and services that come from your most strategic suppliers that is almost always a mistake.

Having the confidence to have your solution shaped by your most strategic partners from the beginning is much more likely to bring you a competitive advantage. This needs to become a habit. Inviting suppliers by way of habit to internal meetings where new ideas and concepts are discussed is a common way of doing this. These are not the quarterly review sessions we talked about previously that are set up specifically for the supplier, these are the company's own meetings that would happen anyway. Of course, the relationship must have reached a high level of trust for this to happen well, but that is what companies that lead in strategic supplier management do.

Visibility of future plans is very similar to early engagement. I have an acquaintance who was in charge of Engineering at a software company, and he gives a good analogy to demonstrate this point. He has been working with a key client for three years and now supplies them with several software modules that help them run some of their core processes and have been built specifically for them. It's automated a lot of what was previously manual and has led to big productivity gains.

However, he said the last three years have been extremely painful. He has had to do significant reconfiguration in that time to ensure different modules feed into each other efficiently and, even though the current solution is generally seen as a success today, it is built in such a way that it would be almost impossible to make even the smallest of changes. That is not good for the client, as business needs will inevitably evolve.

When I asked him why that was, he said, "It's like the client told me to build a table over three years. Only they didn't say, 'Build me a table in three years'. They first told me to build one leg. I didn't know it was going to be a table leg so built a chair leg. Then they told me to build another leg. But because we didn't know it was a leg for the same bit of furniture as the first one, we built it differently, sort of like a different height. Then they told us to build some brackets, then a tabletop, and so on." By the time he realized what he was actually building was a table then, he said, had he known this from day one, he would have built everything very differently to serve the function of a table.

This is an oversimplified example, of course, but how many companies out there really share the entirety of their plans with the strategic suppliers? Again, it's something that requires high levels of trust in a relationship but, by sharing that detailed forward look, suppliers themselves can set themselves up and have their own roadmap to specifically support those plans and not those of your competitors. *And that is what gives you a competitive advantage.*

A final characterization that was implicit in Efficio's survey, but that should probably be called out separately, is aligned incentives. This is fundamental to any strategic relationship. But it's interesting how hard this can be in practice, and it can only really happen with your most strategic suppliers. Having truly aligned incentives means being all in, and that means being prepared to sign up to things over which you have less and in some cases no control.

I know a technology company that had a strategic supplier that was incentivized and paid based on the company's official customer service score. Many of the elements that made up this score were certainly influenceable by the performance of the supplier, but there was a significant number that were not. You also have some of the large consultancies these days, for example McKinsey, getting paid for their transformation programs based purely on corporate share price gains. These types of strategic incentive alignments mean that inefficiencies caused by two parties working on two even mildly competing priorities is minimized and provides a solid basis for the building of trust.

Beware the RFP

Now that we have dealt with the mindset required to run strategic partnerships with suppliers, I want to return to the identification and indeed selection of these parties and the mindset required there, too. And this is where we must give a strong health warning to the usually trusty RFP and supplier onboarding process. Two health warnings, in fact.

As we have talked about in the sourcing chapter, the RFP can be an incredibly effective tool in selecting the right suppliers to serve your organization. But any shortcomings it has are amplified when applied to areas or categories in which strategic suppliers could be found.

The first health warning is about including incumbent strategic suppliers in an RFP. This is not about whether to include or not include. You should, because strategic supplier spend areas are, by definition, ones with high levels of scrutiny, and it is therefore critical they are subject to continuous market scanning and review. But the difference when running an RFP in a strategic spend area is that it absolutely cannot be an arms-length process, run by anyone but your highest-performing cross functional team.

Don't use templates, don't make it a box ticking exercise. The RFP, in this case, is a joint problem-solving exercise between you and the strategic supplier, plus any competitors. If a CPO ever needed to be personally present in an RFP process, this is the one!

The second health warning is about applying an RFP to an area where you might find your next strategic supplier—particularly for industries in which barriers to entry are low and start-ups abound. It is these start-ups that are driving innovation and have the ability to allow their clients to steal a march on the competition.

The reality is that most start-ups and a lot of mid-sized companies simply do not have the capability or capacity to go through an onerous RFP process and respond to an RFP document that is written entirely by the client to collect lots of information, quite a lot of which is not relevant. Even if the suppliers did have the capacity and capability, then often they are precluded from winning the business because of Procurement policies that state a minimum number of reference cases are required, or certain risk scores needed, or other things that will give the largest established suppliers a huge advantage. Quite frankly a company's risk appetite can be the single biggest thing that holds them back from finding that next successful partnership.

The RFP process ends up becoming less a tool to select the next strategic supplier but rather a barrier between the client and that supplier. Procurement really needs to challenge why it runs a particular type of desktop-based RFP in situations where future strategic relationships are at stake and the sort of information it often insists on collecting.

How much do you want to start a relationship with what could be the most important supplier you work with for the next five years by getting them to play a box-ticking game to your rules and your rules only? And normally with these desktop-based RFPs the response, when it is submitted, goes into a black hole as far as the supplier is concerned, and they often don't get any indication of how the bid and proposal have gone down until someone from Procurement phones to tell them yes or no. Not how you want to kick things off with potentially your most important supplier.

This can become a huge cost of doing business for suppliers, especially the smaller ones, and it is why in some instances running RFPs with suppliers is wholly inappropriate—at least the common desktop-based ones.

What Procurement functions should be doing instead is treating future suppliers with an investor mindset. And this could hardly be more different to a desktop-based RFP. Having an investor mindset means wanting the supplier to succeed and lowering the barriers to collaboration as much as possible. It means, for example, involving them in the evaluation process before deciding to invest in them, which could be getting them to shape an RFP if you really are intent on running an RFP. But it also means doing away with the notion that a contract signed at the end of a selection process is the only way that describes how the parties are going to work together in future. A lot of buying organizations think like this and treat the contract as such. That's the equivalent of getting to the end of a sourcing process, as we will discuss in Chapter 9: Savings Realization, and assuming the savings you got signed off at that point with Finance are going to be 100% realized with no further intervention or work required.

No, for the benefits to be realized, then the sign off (or in this case the supplier contract) is just the start! Significant time is required after that point to ensure the benefits of a new supplier relationship flow through. And that is going to require flexibility. This could be changing your Procurement process to enable proof of concept phases for suppliers and therefore iterations of the solution they are going to be providing to your business, further lowering the barriers to cooperation.

Some companies have mastered the art of the investor mindset, of looking at the potential for suppliers and the relationships they could bring, rather than simply considering who is established today, or taking that snapshot-in-time approach we discussed at the beginning of this chapter. It is not uncommon for these companies to have a department specifically targeted at finding start-ups. These departments also work to lower barriers to collaboration with these suppliers, both during the selection phase and by having much more agile and iterative working practices with these suppliers that can be seen in the sorts of relationships we talked about previously.

In summary, the Procurement function often still has too much of an arms-length approach to suppliers, whether strategic of otherwise. A bit like: "I tell you what I want, and you give me your price in a sealed envelope." And once the selection has been made, in some mysterious black box process, there is an assumption that all the prices and promises made by the supplier in the selection process are just going to somehow magically materialize with no effort to embed new ways of working.

This is antiquated and will not allow you to get the best service from your suppliers, much less that competitive advantage from those most strategic partners. What is required is a new mindset, one that seeks to nurture partnerships, wish success for the other party as much as your own, and develop a truly collaborative approach to business problem solving at all levels of the relationship.

8

NON-SAVINGS PRIORITIES:
Balancing Your Objectives

Is There More to Procurement than Savings?

Throughout this book, we have talked about the importance of savings in Procurement. Many of the chapters are dedicated to this topic, whether it's sourcing execution, measuring savings, or how to set your operating model and team up to achieve them. But should Procurement have targets that transcend the savings goals that have been the focus so far? How much territory and remit should Procurement realistically aspire to?

Well, in the second chapter of this book (Ambition), we made our views clear that we think Procurement should ensure it builds its credibility first through delivering savings to the business and deploying commercial rigor. However, we also made the point, and indeed offered some case studies, on Procurement functions that were thinking and acting outside of this remit having already established their savings credibility, for example supporting product development. Going beyond savings is definitely something that mature Procurement functions can aspire to.

But what is the exhaustive list of all these non-savings goals for companies that have already proved they can deliver year-on-year savings? We need to be clear at this point. While we believe there are many non-savings goals, that does not mean they should have no financial value, or even little financial value. In the private sphere at least, companies exist to be profitable and can go about that however they wish while adhering to all relevant laws and regulations. Of course, in the public sector, organizations are not run for profit and must pursue goals in line with the policies of the government of the day.

We make this clear up front, because we think it is important that Procurement functions, as far as the private sector is concerned, do not lose sight of their responsibility to contribute to the financial performance of their company. This is where Procurement functions can deviate from savings, because savings are not the only measure of financial performance.

Consult the Business First

Go into any well-run business—and even most less well-run ones—and they will all have their mission statements with the supporting three to five pillars of success. This mission and its supporting pillars will have been set by the management team and developed specifically to ensure value to the shareholders. And that normally means growth and increased profit. How a company achieves growth and profit will vary wildly from company to company. In a company with a strong and competent executive, the mission and supporting pillars will drive the direction and prioritization in the business. They will have been translated into goals and targets for each function and cascaded down through individual teams.

So, assuming Procurement has already established itself as a competent partner that can deliver savings and is on the lookout for other causes, consulting the business on what Procurement's next gig should be is key, because it needs to pick something that the business cares about and is working towards. A CPO plucking his or her pet topic out of the air as something they want to focus on and be famous for, with no consultation with the business, is a sure-fire way to isolation and failure.

That is not to say that a CPO can't try to influence what a company strives for and help to set the agenda, but it is to say that simply pursuing a topic that is not firmly, and we mean firmly, on the radar of everyone else is not a good idea. We've already talked in this book, specifically in the first two chapters, how important getting clarity of scope and remit is for Procurement. We repeat here what we said there, *Procurement needs to be realistic about what it aims for.*

Consulting the business and understanding its priorities is a good place to start. As we have said, if the business is well-run, these priorities will be linked to the mission of the company, which will bring improved financial performance. Essentially, this is how to arrive at the company's specific Procurement balanced scorecard.

The Procurement Balanced Scorecard

As we have just noted, businesses operate in very different industries and markets, so each has its own unique set of priorities to ensure its success that Procurement can support. But there are some common priorities many companies have that are driven by regulations, societal trends, and customer behaviour. Each of these, if focused on by Procurement, can be traded for Procurement savings to build the Procurement balanced scorecard. And, in some cases, it may not even be a case of trading—it can be possible to make savings while improving a broader range of KPIs linked to other targets.

Here, we take a brief look at just three of the priorities upon which Procurement can have the most impact. Actually, these are not just areas that Procurement has its best chance of impacting, Procurement is ideally placed to play a leading role given its unique position of natural proximity to both the business and supply base!

Sustainability

Sustainability is not new. As a concept it has been around for decades but was previously under the banner of the broader term Corporate Social Responsibility (CSR). In this book we are going to define sustainability with reference to the Triple Bottom Line of environmental, social, and financial sustainability.

Sustainability is increasingly on the agenda of corporations big and small. The reasons are numerous. Governments and international bodies have in recent years introduced swaths of regulation to which companies must adhere, aimed at tackling the latest environmental challenges. Non-compliance can lead to fines or being unable to do business with certain companies or be members of associations.

Some companies have gone further than the regulations require, whether to keep up with their competitors, differentiate themselves in the market, or simply for PR purposes. And many other companies, especially in the era of social media, are desperate to avoid reputational damage amongst their customers by not keeping up with their ever-changing expectations. So, depending on the company and sector, there can be strong economic and financial arguments to be made for having a sustainability agenda.

So how can Procurement help here? Well, the majority of activity that would impact a company's sustainability performance happens in the supply chain with its suppliers. Whether that is working directly with Tier 1 suppliers and their own practices, or building visibility of suppliers' suppliers, Procurement can shine a light on the practices that exist beyond the boundaries of its company, but which the company directly or indirectly supports through its business. And the potential goes further still.

It is by tapping into the supply market that new product innovations can be found that support a company's sustainability agenda. In summary, it's by working with the supply chain that most companies will be able to make the biggest difference on the sustainability topic. And there is no arguing whether that is Procurement's patch! The skills required for this are the same core skills it already possesses for effective supply and demand management, from jointly reviewing specifications to ensuring it's thought about in supplier selection, all the way to managing suppliers and jointly innovating.

Supply chain risk and resilience

You could argue that this one is inherent in a well-run sourcing project and supplier management process. But as COVID-19 has revealed, supply chains today are not as robust as we might have once thought they were. When factories in China shut down for weeks at the beginning of 2020 because of the disease, many companies around the world were left wondering how and when they would get product. With no backup plans to speak of back then, many companies are looking again at their supply chains.

For decades, companies have been outsourcing more and more of their activities, as noted in Chapter 7: Suppliers. While this may have been the right move in terms of focusing companies on their core competencies, there is clearly a price to pay in terms of loss of visibility and control. The issue has been compounded by each layer of the supply chain replicating the outsourcing approach in turn, so that now we have supply chains made up of multiple tiers.

During a crisis such as COVID-19, many companies have seen that their Tier 1 suppliers are only as good as their Tier 2 and 3 suppliers. Critical component shortages with Tier 3 suppliers can bring the production line of a Tier 1 supplier to a grinding halt. Yet, most manufacturing companies have very little transparency or control over those upstream tiers in their supply chains.

At the same time, we've been increasingly globalizing our supply chains, and, as a result, we've become more and more dependent on lower-cost sources from Asia. That's also made the job of getting supplies to our factories more and more complex in terms of transportation, logistics, and lead times.

Now, if we adopt a glass-half-full mindset, then the current crisis has been an opportunity to severely stress-test those setups. And it has revealed weaknesses and pinch-points that we need to work on going forward. Procurement can therefore support the business in answering questions such as: how to make the supply chain more resilient to disruption, how to improve visibility of Tiers 2, 3, and potentially beyond. To what extent should we consider building in more redundancy (e.g. dual rather than single source)? Should we consider more near-shore sourcing, or indeed insourcing, of certain elements?

Obviously, any increase in flexibility in the supply chain comes at a cost, but this is where Procurement can play a leading role. It can help the company to get the balance right by quantifying the trade-offs and ensuring that decisions on prioritization are more data-driven.

Customer service levels and accessing innovation

Enhancing customer satisfaction is at the heart of many companies' missions. With recent technology developments lowering the barriers for suppliers to gain entry to many sectors and markets, and innovative products coming online daily, actively making sure you remain the number one choice for your customer is increasingly important.

We talk in Chapter 7: Suppliers, and also touch upon in Chapter 2: Ambition, that accessing innovation of the key market players is so crucial in maintaining a competitive advantage and being that number one choice for your customers. In the "Suppliers" chapter, we talk about how innovation is not something that just happens because it appears on the agenda of a quarterly business meeting with a supplier. It describes a way of working with the supplier at all levels of the business—right from the top all the way down to the operational day-to-day. This could manifest itself in activities such as dropping by your supplier's factory on a regular basis, visiting their call centers, interviewing their team, asking what they do for their other clients.

Procurement is ideally placed to lead this and, crucially, embed this as business-as-usual practice. This is how strategic supplier relationships are born, and with those relationships you get yourself to the front of the queue when it comes to accessing supplier innovation.

If you take the automotive industry as an example of being so closely aligned with their suppliers—often the result of years of trust that has been built up and on ways of working based on mutual success—companies can profit from benefits, such as exclusive supplier deals or first refusal on a new technology that give a competitive advantage. These are not necessarily innovations that reduce cost and generate savings. They may even increase cost! But by working cross-functionally and understanding what the customers want, Procurement can help to deliver it by tapping into supplier innovation and contribute to the financial success of the company that way.

Procurement does not traditionally get involved in designing the customer experience and accessing innovation, but in some companies—where it is well established—it does, often through playing the role of conduit between the business and suppliers. And where it doesn't, it's often a missed opportunity, because many companies have "bringing innovation to our customers" or "being the partner of choice" as one of the strategic pillars supporting their mission. So, the platform and intent is often there. And, once Procurement has established itself as a credible commercial partner through a savings program, as we keep emphasizing, then this is an area in which it can add significant value.

Sustainability

Of the three areas above, we are going to dive into sustainability simply given the number of companies that now have it as a serious agenda item in their corporate missions. When talking to a colleague a little while ago who specializes in sustainability in Procurement, she remarked how even in the last five years the topic has gone from being slightly fringe—like a nice-to-have for most companies—to now almost all large corporations and many smaller ones having sustainability strategies.

Because so many companies now have sustainability on the agenda, it's important to provide guidance on how to make sure Procurement can help its company ensure that this initiative does not become a box-ticking exercise and that it is a worthwhile and successful initiative. As mentioned earlier, we will treat sustainability here as covering three components: environmental, social, and financial. But the degree to which each of these three is relevant to your business or to individual products and categories will vary.

It's important to note at this point, specifically on environmental sustainability, that while there is broad consensus in the scientific community on the recent warming of the planet, exactly what it will lead to, and even less what the human race could or should do about it, is hotly debated and is more of a political topic than a Procurement one. We do not wish to offer a political viewpoint in this book. Instead, we will work from the perspective that a company has decided that it wants to address sustainability as a means of achieving its broader corporate strategy.

So, let's look at each of the three types of sustainability:

Social sustainability

Ensuring labor practices are ethical, safe, and fair is at the heart of social sustainability. Knowing what happens in your supply chain is critical if you want to mitigate the risk of inadvertently supporting and being associated with unacceptable practices that happen within it, such as exploitative labor in a Tier 3 supplier. This is a common primary focus for businesses to drive transparency and mitigate reputational risks associated with suppliers that use forced or child labor, unsafe production environments, or unethical business practices.

Environmental sustainability

Environmental sustainability focuses on supply, distribution, production, consumption, and disposal of physical goods to avoid or mitigate any detrimental impacts on the environment. Common areas of focus include: building awareness and transparency of natural resources supply (for example, forestry products, or sustainable food production), limiting plastic use, and an increasing awareness of CO_2 footprint within logistics networks.

Environmental sustainability also covers a wide range of additional levers that businesses can pull to improve the sustainability of their Procurement and supply chain, such as utilizing renewable energy sources, limiting waste, and identifying circular economy opportunities through aftermarket sales.

Financial sustainability

This is all about ensuring a business's profit is protected for the long term, even in the event of disruption or market change. Priorities around supply security and price stability are at the forefront of decision making in the wake of major global events, such as the COVID-19 epidemic or natural disasters, linked to the supply chain risk point earlier in the chapter.

In addition to this are more holistic category management reviews around the business's competitive differentiators and ability to serve ever-changing customer requirements, as end-consumers are increasingly aware of, and requiring, sustainable options for purchases.

Get the Right Sustainability Key Performance Indicators

So, what can Procurement do to further the sustainability agenda of its company, assuming it has one? Well, despite sustainability being the big agenda item these days for companies that we've discussed, many businesses are struggling to turn their ambition for better sustainability into tangible results. And this is where Procurement can help. Efficio did a recent survey of top companies, and the single biggest challenge stated in delivering a sustainability program was being unsure how to measure the impact of it (*Starting Your Sustainable Procurement Journey*, October 2020).

This is where having the right KPIs is so important. It allows organizations to identify baselines and priority improvement areas, but also to communicate impacts and trade-offs of critical sourcing decisions. We have found that many businesses view sustainability objectives in isolation from financial and other targets. A strong category or supplier management plan should include a balanced scorecard of cost, quality, and sustainability objectives that can be assessed together, and any trade-off requirements done through conscious decision making.

As is so often the case, it is impossible to come up with one list of KPIs that is suitable for all organizations, as needs and priorities will vary across industries and businesses. But there are some guiding principles that can be applied. These are not unique to Procurement sustainability KPIs, but we will give some examples that are.

The first principle is that the KPI should be clearly measurable and specific to a supplier or category. Where there is a performance ambition but data is not currently collected, new processes and data flags must be put in place to establish a baseline and monitor progress. So, for example, a KPI that states, "plastic-free by 2030" is less effective (less specific and measurable) than one that says, "no single-use plastics used in inbound or outbound packaging materials by 2030." That is because it is easier to put in place a process to track the separate percentages of inbound and outbound products with single-use plastic in the packaging than trying to have a KPI for the first, more vague example.

The second key principle is that the KPI should be outcome-based. For example, we have seen many variations on the sort of sustainability KPI that says "number of suppliers that have been audited" in a particular category. This is all well and good, but this type of KPI simply measures activities being completed from a checklist. A much more effective and outcome-based KPI for the category would read, "percentage of suppliers with an annual spend greater than $100k with successful environmental audit results." This way you are able to measure the actual outcome of what you want, not an input that might not end up giving the desired outcome.

And finally, as is the theme of this chapter, the KPIs need to be aligned to business objectives! If a business objective is to be carbon neutral by 2030, then having a KPI that measures the "logistics CO_2 footprint" is much more effective than something that is not as easy to translate into the overall business objective like, "percentage of suppliers with environmental ISO accreditation." The latter might be a good KPI in isolation, but how does it help the business achieve its stated corporate goals? Without this tight alignment of corporate goals to Procurement's sustainability KPIs it will be harder to get the business's energy and resources focused on Procurement's KPIs.

With these principles in mind, Procurement can support the business to build the appropriate portfolio of sustainability KPIs. When it comes to environmental sustainability, KPIs should be defined to drive transparency and action across each step of the value chain that we spoke about earlier in this chapter: in supply (Does a product come from a renewable, no-conflict, sustainable source? Are we comfortable with how the product was handled and manipulated between original resource acquisition and our supply chain?); distribution (What is the carbon footprint of getting products to and from our suppliers and customers?); consumption (Are we using virgin materials versus recycled or aftermarket options?); production (Are we using sustainable energy and / or water sources? Can we use less?); and disposal (How much are we sending to landfill? How much is recycled or reclaimed?).

But more than simply building this portfolio, Procurement is ideally placed to track progress against it using its unique position close to the supply base. This is where, after having established itself already in the business through a successful savings program, it will have many of the supplier relationships and sophistication of methods and tools to make the tracking of these KPIs much more efficient and effective.

Embarking on Your Sustainability Program

Once, having consulted the business, you have taken on sustainability as part of your Procurement balanced scorecard and then defined your set of effective KPIs, you will need to embark on a sustainability program.

As we have said previously in this chapter, in our experience most companies get themselves to this point but then struggle to operationalize their plan and make an impact. There are some key success factors that we are going to talk about at this point. Perhaps unsurprisingly, some of these success factors are similar and linked to the success factors of a generic program, but with some important specifics.

The first is one we have mentioned already, but it is important enough to be repeated. There needs to be a financial business case for sustainability. Exactly what that is based on will vary significantly from company to company. It could be avoiding regulatory fines. It could be mitigating loss of reputation, or indeed enhancing it further. Or it could be directly related to cost improvements through using less material in production, for example.

It can be tempting to embark on sustainability because "it is the right thing to do," and many people are passionate about the topic. But without a financial business case, it is likely to become secondary to the primary financial targets of the business—at least in the profit-driven private sector. By taking a data-driven and fact-based approach and leveraging core existing Procurement skills like negotiation and demand challenge, you significantly increase the likelihood of your program surviving and being successful, as the emotional and subjective opinions are removed. This data-driven approach needs to shine a light on and quantify the trade-offs between sustainability and other potentially competing measures in the overall Procurement balanced scorecard, such as pure cost savings, for example.

The other advantage of aligning the sustainability topic to broader business targets is ensuring it becomes a business-as-usual activity for *other* functions and teams, as well as Procurement. Without this, sustainability in Procurement, or indeed any program, risks becoming a checkbox exercise to which other functions pay lip service.

The second success factor is also one we have hinted at so far and involves having a highly skilled Procurement function. This goes beyond Procurement having established itself in the business through the savings program, though that is a prerequisite. It means that the Procurement function is adept at skillfully evaluating, selecting, and managing suppliers, as well as effectively challenging demand and working with operations on requirements. Given that achieving the KPIs we have already talked about will not be possible without having the right suppliers and managing them correctly, it's not hard to see how a Procurement function that has honed its experience in this area is key.

And finally, strong sponsorship is particularly important for any sustainability program. This is not something that can be delivered entirely by Procurement. As per one of the enduring themes of this book, it is a cross-functional endeavor that requires people in Engineering, Logistics, Operations, and other functions to play their part to ensure success; for example, through buying into new specifications and ways of working and positively supporting the conversations with the supply base. Having a governance structure that allows the program to hold individuals to account for achieving their share of the goals is essential.

At the beginning of this chapter, we asked if there was more to Procurement than savings. Subsequently, we have made the point that there is, but care is needed. Ensuring a foundational layer of credibility on savings earns you the right to expand Procurement's remit, as we also argued in Chapter 2: Ambition. But that is not the only pitfall. Ensuring the additional focus is aligned to corporate objectives and makes a financial contribution is critical, as the business case will help the initiative become part of business as usual. For many businesses, one of these new objectives is sustainability, but it is not the only one, and Procurement is ideally placed to drive a sustainability program given its proximity to the business and suppliers.

9

SAVINGS REALIZATION:
Stemming the Leaks

"I'm just trying to understand what happened to those Procurement savings."

"Which ones?" said CPO, John.

"The damn $75m you promised me for this year, John. I can just about find $25m, but that's it! This is not what I needed at this point. I was counting on those savings, John."

Sound like a familiar CFO to CPO conversation at year-end time? Yep. All too familiar, unfortunately.

This is clearly not a good outcome for anybody: the CFO doesn't get his / her savings, and the CPO loses all credibility. After all, savings are one of his or her most concrete deliverables, and the CFO would argue that what he / she has submitted is not valid. This dynamic often goes on for years, along with an inside joke about "Procurement savings." Ultimately, all the good work of Procurement will come to nothing if the savings can't be found, or simply never materialize.

While technically much of the work associated with savings measurement and budgeting sits with Finance, clearly Procurement has a central part to play. It has to deliver real savings, it has to provide evidence of its existence, and it has to help ensure that the organization is compliant, and the savings are actually realized.

The importance of "savings" to Procurement cannot be underestimated. If sourcing is the engine room of Procurement, then savings are the lifeblood. And yet ... people get it so wrong. So, let's take a look at what seems to make the topic of savings so difficult (it's almost a dirty word!), and let's see if we can maybe help make it a little easier.

We'll look at what constitutes a "saving;" we'll look at how to track it through its various stages; and we'll consider the various leakage points that contribute to turn a $100 negotiated saving into a $10 realized saving.

What Is a Saving?

Let's start with some definitions that are important when it comes to savings. So, what is a saving?

A saving is a reduction in cost versus current or historical costs. In Procurement, it can take a number of forms: we can reduce the price of the item, we can swap the item for a more cost-effective specification (for example, moving from branded parts to generic parts), we can receive an annual rebate or other incentives from the supplier, we can link our purchases to an index to ensure we're not overpaying versus the market, and we can effect a total cost of ownership saving (for example, by buying a more expensive but much more efficient pump). All of these are valid.

Procurement is *not* just about price reduction. I've had a number of clients over the years try to tell me that, if the specification is changed, Procurement can't claim credit! I guess it goes back to what we said about Procurement's remit, but of course these savings count.

So, what doesn't count? Business-driven volume changes, for one thing. If you close one of your three factories, you might reduce your Facilities Management expenses by a third ... but that's clearly not a Procurement-driven cost reduction.

Market-driven commodity price changes are also not defensible ... but the same applies if the market price goes up, in which case Procurement should not be penalized. Which leads us to the gray area of cost avoidance. This is simply where you *avoid* a price increase that you would otherwise have had to absorb. In our opinion, there will be isolated instances where cost avoidance is indeed valid but, for the most part, we would advise against trying to claim credit for cost avoidance savings. A cost avoidance is a weak saving and will dilute the credibility of the rest of the savings unless there is a rock-solid case.

Beyond this, any quantifiable cost reduction should be fair game. Notice the word "quantifiable" though; and to be in a position to quantify something, you must first have dependable data.

The Importance of Data and Baselining

We discussed the topic of baseline-building in detail in Chapter 3: Sourcing Execution. The standard, simplified savings calculation, which requires customization at the category level, is based on the formula: Annual Volume times (Old Price minus New Price). The new prices will come from the suppliers as part of their RFP responses, so the elements to get right in the baselining are the volumes and the current prices (as well as the specifications, which must facilitate an apples-to-apples comparison). Depending on the category, your baseline may need to be based on a sample of the spend, which must be large enough and carefully constructed to represent the entire spend.

Of course, none of this data is readily available. People often think that the Purchase Order system or the ERP system should have this level of data but, especially when it comes to indirect costs, it doesn't.

These systems won't tell us how many parts we bought at which price, which is what we need. This data will have to be obtained from Operations in the case of Cost of Goods Sold. In the case of indirects, the work-around to getting item-level data is to request it from the suppliers—it's their revenue, so they have very granular data, and are usually willing to provide it if asked as part of an RFP process. For a CPO, creatively finding data, and securing the necessary analytical support to manipulate it, are absolute core competences.

Data also becomes critical at the point of signing off the savings. If executed properly, the Strategic Sourcing process should naturally produce a rich and reliable data set, in terms of line items consumed annually, and current and supplier bid pricing. This data is key to creating a credible savings business case that can be signed off by Finance.

This savings business case can become quite complex, depending on the category. For example, you may need to ring-fence or strip out non-controllable commodity costs before measuring savings; or you may need to factor in total cost of ownership savings that go beyond the base formula of Old Price minus New Price. All of these require good quality data that needs to be collected during the baselining and bidding phases of the sourcing process.

Savings Need to Be Delivered Before They Can Be Measured

Now that we're clear on definitions and on the need for good data and baselining, let's get back to savings. Of course, savings need to be *delivered* first, before they can be articulated, measured, and realized.

When it comes to savings delivery, we've talked at length about how that needs to come through proper Strategic Sourcing. There is a difference between fundamental cost reductions and "BAU (Business as Usual) savings." BAU savings are typically a hodge-podge of things, some more bankable than others. It's basically anything anyone can articulate, and it's thrown in the mix.

BAU savings include discounts off supplier list prices, improvement of Quote 1 versus Quote 2, improvement versus budget, cost avoidance (including the avoidance of proposed supplier price increases), one-off discounts associated with large orders, and more. Some of these then, will be *impossible* to find in the P&L, because they were mere constructs (e.g., Bid 2 versus Bid 1) that make no difference in what we spend in reality.

So, it pays (pardon the pun) to harvest what we would call "structural savings"—savings that come from fundamentally re-setting the cost base, by doing something differently and on an annualized or even multi-year basis; savings that encompass the total spend and take a total cost perspective.

For example, "outsourcing our Facilities Management services to a Tier 1 FM partner across Europe," "strategically sourcing our machined metal parts from a network of 13 approved global suppliers with dynamic volume allocation," or even "strategically sourcing Travel by agreeing and implementing a strict new global travel policy, appointing a new global travel agency partner, and putting in place airline route deals, a global car rental deal, and two preferred hotels for all core locations." Now *that's* what I call a *saving*! And these types of savings come through Strategic Sourcing, as discussed elsewhere in this book.

So, Step 1 is to deliver, operationally if you like, the savings. Step 2 is to articulate, measure, and realize those savings—two separate but linked challenges.

The CFO Needs to Be Procurement's Best Friend

When it comes to articulating and measuring numbers, who in the organization is good at that? Let me think ... Finance! If Procurement can get Finance in its corner, it'll be onto a winner. Finance must not be the enemy asking for answers about non-materialized savings, but the friend who is there every step of the way, who understands, can vouch for, and can ultimately "budgetize" the savings.

Finance should play a key part at certain points in the sourcing process, for instance in signing off on the baseline (today's spend), signing off on supplier bid comparisons, and, ultimately, signing off on the saving and, hopefully, removing it from budgets.

The best way to engage Finance with Procurement is to do so early and often. And the best way to do that is for Finance to be a formal part of the Procurement Governance Organigram, or the Program Organization Chart for the Procurement transformation program.

This should be a high-caliber, well-connected Procurement Controller, who is implanted full time to the effort. He or she works across all the sourcing teams to intimately understand all the numbers from Day One—the spends, the baselines, the price points, the savings opportunities. Such an approach makes the sign off and budgeting of savings at the end, infinitely easier.

Also, numbers are cheap these days! So, if you're going to pursue a Strategic Sourcing or Procurement transformation agenda, a key deliverable of which is sourcing savings, then you'd better know what you're doing numbers-wise. It's as much about what you communicate as it is about what you actually save.

We recommend "tracking" or "progressing" savings targets from inception through to savings realization in the P&L; that's one hell of a journey! So, savings would then be classified as: Target, Identified, Negotiated, Contracted, Signed-off, Implemented, Budgeted, and Realized (TINCSIBR)—eight stages, which admittedly is quite a few.

But that's from start to finish. And the advantage of tracking the savings over time is that it creates momentum, especially when sourcing a number of competing categories simultaneously. It also again brings to life the category portfolio effect, as some categories' numbers go up while others go down, while hopefully the cross-category aggregate result remains intact.

TINCSIBR

Let's take a brief look at each of the stages in that TINCSIBR (not much of a catchphrase) journey, by explaining each of the savings stages. The idea is to have all categories start at the Target stage and then move forward at different paces, so that you focus on moving all the teams from the left to the right. It makes for a great sourcing program tracking tool—"Savings by Savings Stage." Right, so let's look at each one in turn (see Figure 9.1).

TINCSIBR Savings Progression over Time

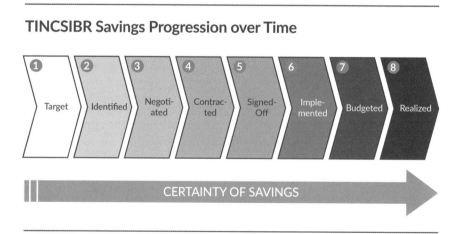

Figure 9.1   TINCSIBR Savings Progression over Time

TARGET: This is the program target, likely made up of a number of category savings targets. This does not change over time; it is set in stone. It should be expressed as a range (Low, Mid, High)—for example, 7%, 12%, 15% for a "standard" indirect category like Travel, or 2%, 3%, 4% for a commodity chemical in scarce supply.

IDENTIFIED: This comes during "Steps 1 to 3" of the sourcing process (see Chapter 3: Sourcing Execution). It's when we have built up a category strategy and can therefore better estimate the true addressable scope and the exact nature of the savings opportunities. It serves as a validation of the Target savings, but comes before any supplier bids are received so is unconfirmed at this point ... "our best guess until the bids come in."

NEGOTIATED: We can count negotiated savings at any point from the return of supplier bids and during supplier negotiations. It's what has been negotiated thus far; it's "in the bag" if we want it, but there may be more to come. The reason it's relevant is that it shows the eagerly awaited first savings being evidenced in supplier bid responses. Good for team morale.

CONTRACTED: These are the savings that we project, based on expected future volumes times (Old Price minus New Price). It's the savings the suppliers agree to in their final pricing. This is often the point at which savings measurement stops in companies. Contracted savings are colloquially known as "paper savings," and that's correct—its signed in paper, but has not yet materialized in dollars.

SIGNED-OFF: Finance needs to formally sign off on all savings. Each sourcing team should fill out a template that lays out the spend, the sourcing strategy, the chosen suppliers, and the savings calculation. This form has to be signed off by Finance (the Procurement controller) and by the key stakeholders (e.g., CIO, Manufacturing Director). Proper sign-off helps to legitimize the saving within the organization, and it helps to hold people to account; and it facilitates budget adjustment. Proper sign-off, based on proper supporting evidence, is critical.

IMPLEMENTED: After the savings are CONTRACTED, the deal with the suppliers is done. Now it needs to be implemented, and typically one would see savings coming on stream Business Unit by Business Unit, or country by country, as the new deal is rolled out. I don't need to explain what implementation of the contract looks like; suffice to say, this is where many companies get stuck, with the result that the savings don't move beyond "paper savings."

BUDGETED: Arguably budgeting sits outside the operational savings process, and there are options around *when* in the process it occurs (before or after the sourcing execution), but we include it here for completeness. In non-COGS categories, if you don't take the money out of budgets, it'll just be spent elsewhere, and all the savings will have been for nothing. It's the CFO's task to take the savings out of budgets, and he/she should do so only after discussing the detail of the savings with the CPO. When it comes to budgeting, in our view Procurement's key deliverable is a reliable, accurate savings forecast; the rest is up to Finance.

REALIZED: The holy grail of Procurement! Realized savings! The "R word!" What stands between IMPLEMENTED and REALIZED is compliance, and the key to realizing savings is to drive up compliance. Realized savings are very difficult to articulate in practice, given the macro level effects of extraneous factors, such as business mix changes and volume changes. But if you can prove compliance ("this shows that 80% of the spend is going to the preferred supplier at the right price"), then you have proof of realized savings. At the end of the day, a saving *can* be realized, and it can be proven, but it may never be "P&L-visible."

TINCSIBR. A fairly simple concept then, but few companies measure savings along a continuum like TINCSIBR. They may have a Target, and they may record Contracted and Budgeted savings, but the numbers won't be fully linked.

Using a framework like TINCSIBR (it's catching on now!) helps to manage expectations over time, and it helps to avoid surprises at the end. Numbers develop naturally, as reality diverts from the original plan. Combining the by now famous TINCSIBR framework with the category portfolio effect, we can make light work of the management of expectations around savings. We can have a live roadmap that shows the status of each category, and the magnitude of savings at each stage. This creates excitement and momentum and, in the really successful sourcing programs I've seen, competition across category teams. A virtuous cycle, driving the categories forward. Simple but powerful stuff.

It's All About Compliance

Another dreaded word ... compliance. What we're talking about is compliance to the sourcing deals that you've worked so hard to put in place. The problem with compliance is that, in many instances, Procurement intervenes to conduct a sourcing event (or renew a contract), and then pulls out, way before compliance or non-compliance can even manifest themselves.

There is an assumption that there will be savings, there is an assumption that everyone will adopt the new supplier, and that the new supplier will actually honor the pricing promised in the RFP response. But nobody checks! And the reason nobody checks is that the Procurement guys pull out after the sourcing is done, and the budget-holder is not all that bothered about the savings detail.

In fact, it's extremely common for the ongoing management of categories and of suppliers to completely fall between two stools in organizations. No wonder then, that your compliance to that new deal is only 27%!

So, how exactly should you go about compliance management? Well, there's no magic bullet but, in a nutshell, you check with Accounts Payables to find out which suppliers the money has gone to in a particular category, and then you follow up as to why. The problem lies in the following up, because the compliance mechanism often has no teeth in practice.

The classic one is Travel, where I've seen numerous examples of companies tracking who violates the class-of-air-travel policy ... only to bury the evidence when they find out that the CEO, the CFO, and the Manufacturing Director are the biggest culprits on the offenders list. When companies do get it right, it's on a naming-and-shaming basis. If we've all signed up to a certain policy, we shouldn't be breaking it, and we should be OK with being shamed (or to comply out of fear of being shamed).

It works, you just have to bite the bullet and do it. In the Travel example, extreme best practice is when you simply don't reimburse for the non-compliant expense item. You don't follow the rules, you don't get paid back! Now, that's teeth.

I remember doing a pan-European Office Supplies deal for a large insurance brokerage. We signed the deal just before Christmas, and in January we immediately knew something wasn't working. Luckily we had had the foresight to put in place a compliance tracking team, and they spent the next three months asking the following questions (the three elements of compliance): (i) Are we buying from the selected supplier, and if not, who is not, and what is the reason? (ii) Are we buying the correct items, i.e., the "core items list" of 300 items, for which we have special discounts? (iii) Is the supplier applying the right price, the price that they promised us in their RFP submission?

It took three months to get the three metrics from "terrible" to "good!" Not only were users ordering from their previous suppliers, and we were not ordering off the preferred items list … but the supplier was not giving us the preferential pricing we agreed, because the supplier himself could not enforce his globally agreed prices across his country business units! Lots of checking, lots of back and forth, three months of hard work, for … Office Supplies. (By the way, if we keep mentioning Office Supplies, Travel, and MRO Materials in this chapter, it's for a reason: these categories involve a large number of dispersed users buying a large number of items, making compliance particularly difficult.)

Tracking and managing compliance can be hard work, as it relies on a number of disparate data elements coming together. However, these days much can be done to automate the process if technology is intelligently deployed.

I remember us helping a large water utility to source its Capex spend—essentially billions of dollars' worth of construction spend associated with maintaining the water infrastructure. Using simple Tableau-based technology, we built the client a sophisticated Cost Management System for tracking all prices and costs across the whole network of construction partners across the country. It was extremely powerful, as it enabled the company to track compliance in real time across a large number of regions, construction projects, and suppliers.

In this instance, the suppliers themselves entered and maintained their costing data, subject to periodic audits, thereby further automating the process for the client. With current technology, it can be surprisingly easy to build a workable solution around what may at first seem an intractable challenge.

Effective Budgeting

Budgeting is a process that exists in a parallel world to the operational buying process, and we need to be mindful of it throughout. In theory, after the savings are implemented, Procurement has done its part, and it's now over to Finance. Then again, it's surely in Procurement's interest to stay involved and see the savings through to the end.

We've seen that compliance management is a difficult task. We've also seen that the measurement of savings is difficult, as ERP systems are limited in their ability to track savings at the order, item, quantity, and price level.

Budgeting for savings is arguably an even more difficult art form. On the COGS side, where parts are itemized in the budget and ERP system, it's relatively straightforward, as the money drops straight to the bottom line. But across indirect costs, it's much more difficult because the costs are allocated to budgets at a summary level.

Imagine you did a great deal with Staples for Office Supplies for your company, saving you 23% on stationery. If you didn't adjust anybody's budget, you would not save a penny as an organization. If there is a Procurement saving and it doesn't get taken out of a budget, we call it a windfall. Which is a bad thing. Why save money and then willy-nilly squander it elsewhere just because you can?

Budgeting is really a Finance topic. In the context of Procurement, the key thing that matters is *when* the money comes out of budgets. In an ideal world, the financial haircut should come *before* Procurement is set loose, rather than after the fact ... so as to position the function as a helper to the budget-holder rather than as the bad guy who saves you money, then gives it away to Corporate.

Whether or not to take the money before the event depends on the amount of faith the CFO has in the CPO and his/her ability to deliver. In a well-oiled CFO–CPO relationship, that trust is there, making the budgeting process that much easier.

The other issue in budgeting is the mechanics of (i) matching operational savings to budget lines (where do they hit?), and (ii) determining whether the saving is already spoken for (in which case all you can deliver is an "underpin"). Again, this is more an issue for Finance to figure out.

What we have seen many times, is budget-holders resisting incremental savings targets by arguing that the savings were already baked into other, ongoing initiatives. My recommendation would be that if there isn't any clear evidence of a workstream addressing the *external spend element*, then the saving is actually incremental, rather than budget underpin. The best advice when it comes to budgeting—*get Finance involved early and often*. Bringing them in at the end is not going to work, trust me.

Savings Leakage Points

So, what ever did happen to "those savings you promised me?" Did the savings just not happen, despite being reported? Or did they happen and just cannot be pinpointed in the P&L? Well, as with most things in life, there isn't a single, simple answer. Rather, there are a number of what we call "savings leakage points" along the journey that's followed by a saving as it travels from supplier price negotiation to P&L account, as illustrated in **Figure 9.2**.

These leakage points combine to erode the saving, and the more of them we can plug, it stands to reason, the smaller we can make the delta between our "paper savings" and what's eventually realized.

But before we look at each of these leakage points in turn, let's take a step back and consider why savings measurement and identification seems to be such a difficult thing. Surely, it's simple to articulate, "what I paid last time versus what I'm paying now," so where is the problem?

Let's use a hypothetical example. Let's imagine that, in a mid-sized Manufacturing company, the buyer for MRO (Maintenance, Spares, and Operating Supplies), which includes such factory supplies as

Savings Leakage Points

Why Do Savings Not Hit the P&L?

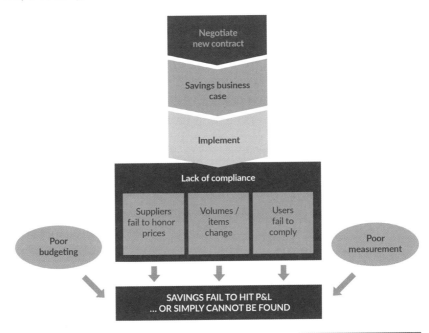

Figure 9.2   Savings Leakage Points

valves, pumps, motors, bearings, tools, pipes, and nuts and bolts, has just inked a new deal with an MRO distributor.

The buyer has followed a structured sourcing process—he has articulated last year's baseline down to the price paid for each and every nut and bolt; he has agreed with Manufacturing to harmonize the number of products used, so that instead of using 3,000 SKUs, there is now a new parts list of only 800 core items; he has negotiated favorable prices for each of these items; and he has produced a document that calculates the annual savings, showing that the coming year's cost across the 800 items is 27% lower than last year's cost of buying 3,000 line items.

It's a great result; the contract with the supplier is signed and, as far as the buyer is concerned, his work is done … may the money begin flowing in! If only it were that simple though. For a start, the definition of the "saving" in this instance is actually quite difficult.

What the buyer is telling us is that the 27% is "the difference between what we *would* have spent *if* we had bought at last year's prices, and what we *think* we're *going* to spend next year, *assuming* that we will buy a similar volume, and that we actually buy off the harmonized items list rather than continuing to buy the items we buy today." Plenty of assumptions then, which means plenty of things that can go wrong.

Even if we buy exactly as planned, one could argue that the saving is still predicated on the assumption that if we hadn't made the saving, we would have bought at last year's prices. But what if steel prices crashed and sent MRO prices nose-diving? Then the savings inherent in the new deal would suddenly look much smaller.

The point is that a "saving" in this context is a somewhat theoretical construct based on a number of assumptions ... so even before we start to look at what happens to the MRO savings in reality, we need to recognize that, whatever happens, the one thing that's for sure is that the numbers *will* change.

But let's get back to our leakage points. The first leakage point is the savings calculation, or the savings business case. This is the buyer's calculation of projected "baseline cost versus new cost," as discussed earlier. Clearly, if this is erroneous, then the savings figure will also be wrong. So, it's important to get this right—which means basing it on very granular volume and pricing data, and making assumptions that stand up to scrutiny.

The next leakage point comes during implementation. The savings will not materialize in their entirety if the deal is not properly implemented. This includes making sure that the new deal is fully communicated to all business units / divisions, that the buying channels and ordering mechanisms are set up, and that the supplier is clear on what products are to be delivered to whom and at what price. Failure to complete any of these tasks properly will lead to the company continuing to buy from the wrong suppliers or at the wrong price points.

But even if the contract is properly implemented, there will be compliance issues that need to be proactively managed if the full savings are to be harvested. In fact, it is not uncommon to lose more than half the savings through lack of compliance. Compliance has a number of elements, including vendor compliance, price compliance, and item compliance.

In our MRO example, some of the company's factories will likely continue to buy from their existing suppliers rather than from the new suppliers (vendor non-compliance), or they may continue to buy off-spec parts (item non-compliance). Finally, the supplier itself may be non-compliant, in terms of not honoring the agreed prices (price non-compliance).

Compliance is a major issue for most companies. In most cases, post-contract compliance is simply not measured or managed because it falls between two stools, as already discussed. So, it is simply assumed that the savings will materialize as per the plan, but of course this is naïve. Leading companies implement a proactive compliance measurement and management process to address savings leakage from non-compliance. Left to its own devices, compliance will simply not happen.

Managing compliance is a time-consuming, iterative process that involves (i) identifying instances of non-compliance, (ii) looping back with users to understand the *reasons* for their non-compliance, and (iii) addressing those reasons, and / or taking corrective action as appropriate. Driving compliance involves changing behaviour, which is never easy, and which requires incentives.

Next up in the list of savings leakage points is poor budgeting. Let's assume that the MRO deal has been diligently implemented and compliance has been proactively managed. If this is the case, then there will indeed be a saving. However, if this money is not taken out of budgets, there will just be a windfall. The saving will only actually hit the bottom line once the money is taken out of budgets. This sounds obvious, but is often not done, or not done well. Good CPOs work closely with Finance to make sure that operational savings are translated into budget cuts.

"Poor measurement" is a close cousin of "Poor budgeting." As the saying goes, "you can't have what you can't measure." But of course, doing the budgeting doesn't in any way facilitate the operational saving … this still needs to be diligently tracked and measured. And, once again, companies operate in functional silos, and the ongoing measurement of Procurement savings falls between the cracks. No surprise then, if the savings can't be found in the P&L.

Lastly, business-driven volume or changes in the item mix can obscure the savings delivered, even if they don't actually reduce them. Thus, in our MRO example, if the company opens a new factory, spend will go up and, if the company switches to new machinery that requires more expensive parts, the item mix will be unfavorably impacted. These changes need to be stripped out / corrected for before the P&L saving can be clearly articulated.

Clearly then, there is a lot that can go awry as a saving travels from contract signature to bottom line. Significantly, 50%-plus levels of savings leakage *will* occur if leakage is not proactively managed. In order to do so, companies have to work effectively across functions, i.e., Procurement, Finance, and the budget-holder. Between them, they need to ensure that (i) one of these functions actively monitors and manages compliance, and (ii) Finance takes the money out of budgets.

For this to happen seamlessly, the three functions need to work together from the start, not just when it comes to finding the money at the end. If all parties are involved in the sourcing process from start to finish, then they will jointly agree on the cost baseline, on the supplier volume allocation, and on the compliance picture as it emerges over time. Articulating and capturing the savings then becomes easy.

Key Steps to Stem the Leakage

So, let's quickly summarize to aid with retention. The key steps you can take to minimize savings leakage are as follows:

- Get your savings calculation / business case right, by making sure it is based on granular volume and pricing data, and it makes reasonable assumptions.
- Make sure the supplier contract gets implemented properly, and that all divisions / business units are aware of the new contract and how to buy from it.
- Make someone accountable for measuring and managing vendor, item, and price compliance ... without this, you will fail. Engage Finance early, and ideally have them take the savings out of budgets up front.

- Make sure you measure both budget savings and operational savings, stripping out any extraneous factors, such as business-driven volume or mix changes to the extent possible; use compliance data to prove savings realization.
- Use a system like TINCSIBR to track the evolution of savings by category over time, and to help manage expectations and avoid surprises at the end.

A Procurement function's reputation and credibility lives and dies by the validity of its proclaimed savings. For a CPO, getting this part wrong should really be a firing offence.

Procurement needs to be fully and proactively engaged in the savings measurement process both during and *after* the sourcing process, and it's the CPO's job to make sure that Finance is fully engaged from Day One.

It's all about being proactive. If you wait for the CFO to ask, "Where are those savings?," then you're already too late.

10

TECHNOLOGY: Investing in and Adopting the Right Tools

A Procurement Revolution That Hasn't Happened

The world we inhabit in the 2020s is so vastly different to that of 10 or 20 years ago, even allowing for a global pandemic. And there is one major cause of that. Technology. It has such a profound impact on the way we go about our personal lives, in particular.

Let's look at some examples. Take something as simple as booking a cab. Today, in any major city, you can get your smart phone out, tap a few times, and you'll be picked up within minutes and taken to your destination. All this without needing to talk to another human being or physically give anyone any money. It makes taking a cab so much easier and more convenient. Remember when you had to hail a cab or phone a central number? Then you'd have to say where you wanted to go and hope the driver knew it, which they sometimes didn't, and so you'd have to explain. Finally, you'd be messing about with cash and change in the back of the car in an attempt to pay at the end, because they didn't take credit cards.

Then look at communication. We can now meet with work colleagues, and even attend conferences, all from our own homes. Many predict we will never return to a pre-pandemic world in which most people go into an office every day. Why would we, with all the video technology, online collaboration rooms, and the multiple chat functionality on our devices? Granted, virtual collaboration is not exactly the same as face-to-face, and it can be draining, but it means we don't need to be face-to-face all the time anymore, or even most of the time.

Before all this online collaboration, phoning and conference calling were generally seen as poor substitutes for meeting face-to-face, which is why there was a lot more travelling and commuting. Admittedly, the current global pandemic has changed our attitudes to office working at an accelerated speed, but without the technology this virtual collaborating would not be becoming the new norm.

And finally, since this is a book about Procurement, what about buying something? Let's assume it's something quite complicated like a vacation. Remember the travel agents that populated most town centers just a couple of decades ago? You'd walk in there and browse the brochures of the types of places you'd like to go to. The travel agent might even give you some pointers. You would have to take the brochures home for a few days to flick through and discuss with your partner, then go back to the travel agent, who would phone the holiday companies and airlines on your behalf and book you a trip.

It was quite a lot of work and phoning, checking availability and prices. Do they do family rooms? Is the special tariff valid over the public holiday? Are there good restaurants nearby? What about the dog? The travel agent offered a service doing all that for you—because there was a lot you couldn't do yourself. Or could, but it would have been very time-consuming. But now, where are the travel agents? Well, there are a few still dotted around if you look hard enough. But today they tend to cater for people looking for something very specific, who still enjoy and are prepared to pay for the service a middleman (the travel agent) performs. But mostly travel agents have disappeared from our high streets.

The fact is almost everyone buys holidays and flights themselves these days online. There is huge price transparency online today, meaning you can compare all sorts of pre-sourced deals yourself, without a travel agent. You can check availability of rooms and tours just by clicking a button and without having to phone anyone. You can check with a simple search where all the best restaurants are near the hotel. There are many reviews to read, and overall, they give you a good sense of what you are letting yourself in for and whether it's worth spending all that money. The experience of booking a holiday is so much different from how it used to be. As individuals, we are so much more in control of the process. And it's great!

But what happens when we want to buy something at work? Even something simple? Well, it can sometimes feel like we've stepped into a time warp to 20 or 30 years ago. Depending on the company, you're probably still made to fill out a requisition template or similar, just like you did way before the turn of the century. You then need to send it off to a Procurement function. You might be waiting a few days, or much longer, for a response.

Then, when the response does come, it might tell you not to buy what you wanted but to buy something a bit different. And you have to buy from certain suppliers because they're the ones already in the system—and to set up another one takes a lot of time and more form-filling. Maybe they can't tell you what the lead time will be for the product you want, so they'll have to come back to you on that one. Or perhaps your request just isn't a priority right now, so you've been moved down the queue.

Is it a wonder that people get confused and frustrated with how different Procurement is at work compared to our personal lives? Somebody books a two-week vacation in an evening all by themselves, then the next day they still don't have an answer from Procurement on the four spare parts they're trying to obtain to keep a key piece of manufacturing machinery going!

The reality is that, despite the existence of technologies today to make purchasing so much more streamlined, the corporate world is lagging behind the consumer world by some distance. There is a revolution there that just hasn't happened.

The Steam Powered Tesla

Technology and digital have become buzzwords in many businesses and in Procurement. Procurement functions have digital strategies and are making technology purchases. Clearly people are putting a lot of faith in technology because these systems don't come cheap, with implementation costs that can run into six- or seven-figure sums.

Efficio ran a study in 2018 (*The Future of Procurement*) and asked a few hundred Procurement leaders in Europe and the U.S. the value they ascribed to technology in Procurement. The results were revealing! Almost 80% thought it should be a boardroom priority, and about two-thirds said emerging digital solutions in the space were causing them to completely rethink their approach to Procurement. So clearly technology is on the Procurement agenda! But, amazingly, about 50% of those same respondents admitted to purchasing technology from a fear of missing out rather than understanding the full benefits of what they were buying.

This is a dangerous state of affairs. You essentially have lots of shiny and expensive Procurement technology gadgets on the market and half the Procurement leadership (at least of this particular study) buying them without a full understanding of benefits. Without some caution, there are going to be some wrong technology purchasing decisions. And, trust me, we've seen a few!

Technology is not going to solve a problem or make something better all on its own. Technology is there purely to enable a better operating model, a better way of working. It is part of that better operating model. But without considering the other parts of that operating model—which are mainly people, data, and processes—then you'll remain at square one. Actually, you'll remain at square one having spent money and potentially some goodwill that others had towards you in trusting you to make the technology purchase. This is arguably square *minus* one.

The clearest and simplest example I've seen of a Procurement technology investment gone wrong is when a retail bank decided (correctly) that it needed to get better visibility of its supplier contracts. There was no central place for contracts. They existed on everyone's hard drives or shared drives. Ahead of key negotiations with suppliers, they sometimes couldn't locate the contract. There was also a regulatory angle, and a recent audit by the regulator had recommended that they make improvements in this area.

So, the bank did what you would expect. They bought a contracts repository. And that is what they got. A contracts repository.

Only, 10 months later there is no reliable data coming from the repository—many contracts are not in there, and most of the business does not use it. And we can't even say the technology isn't any good. It is! They bought the solution from a reputable vendor that has a solid technical product. What went wrong? Without being unjustly critical there are some fundamental things that never went right.

Firstly, the Procurement function in this case didn't consider how they would need to change the process of capturing contracts across the bank. What meta data would need to be recorded with each contract to give the visibility they needed? For example, expiry date, contract value, and supplier name. Secondly, they didn't consider how they would get people to use it. And I don't mean just giving them some training on how to use it. Of course, that is necessary, but then you just get lots of people who know how to use it but don't. No, you also need to incentivize people to use it, give them a reason. What are they going to get in return, how can the tool make their life of managing contracts easier, such that they want to use a new tool?

In this case, the Procurement function in question made the classic error that, to be fair to them, many other Procurement functions have made—namely, they built a steam-powered Tesla. The tool itself is great, one of the best in the market. But it doesn't have any fuel in the form of data or usage. So, it never gets going. It sits there idle.

What could they have done differently? They could have designed a new contracts operating model up front, keeping in mind the people, process and data implications. They could have sought better visibility of contracts, compatibility with one of the many technology solutions out there, technology that would slot in to the new model seamlessly and facilitate the improvements they were looking for. Of course, it's always easier to write that in a couple of sentences than to actually do it. But do it we must to get the fuel in place and power whatever technology solution we implement. A Ford with a one-liter engine would have traveled faster and further than a steam-powered Tesla.

Technology's Promise to Procurement

So far, we have established in this chapter that technology is there to support an operating model. And new technology can help support new and better operating models in Procurement. Specifically in Procurement, there are three key ways we see that technology can support a better operating model in the future.

The first and most obvious is automation. Taking Procurement as a whole, the operational activities in the purchase to pay (P2P) part are more feasible to automate because they are more repeatable. However, most companies have not gotten close to automating their P2P, processes yet. But artificial intelligence (AI) already makes this possible. In P2P, there are often a myriad of processes in just one company, and it is not always possible to standardize them due to the need to account for local requirements and to retain flexibility.

AI helps by not only remembering all these processes (which conventional software can do anyway) but being able to translate machine speak into human language and interact with the user. This way it can handle queries and reduce the time it takes for a business user to, say, purchase a component they need. The "bot" can ask the user a series of questions, perhaps relating to volume and specification, and then either raise the order with a preferred supplier or pass it to someone in the upstream sourcing team if no source yet exists.

If the case does get passed there, then the strategic activities in Procurement, such as sourcing and supplier management, are harder to automate completely; but even here, AI can get us some of the way there. For example, it can help to identify new opportunities by analyzing spend and contract data, helping to build a pipeline. It can also help with predictive risk modeling with key suppliers, by trawling the Internet for signals that would impact a risk score and updating the allocated supplier manager. This codification of logic treats Procurement as a science in which logic is programmed into machines that in turn put compelling insights into the hands of decision makers. These decision makers can then make much more effective decisions, no longer needing to either spend all of their day collecting and interpreting data or giving up and just using their hunch or "experience."

Despite AI's potential here, it is important to appreciate that simplifying processes in the first place is a key enabler of automation. AI should not be the first step. Simplifying current processes should be. That will unleash the full potential of AI.

The second major application of technology in Procurement is communication—between suppliers and the businesses trying to buy their services or products. Business-to-business (B2B) marketplaces are still lagging behind their business-to-consumer (B2C) counterparts (such as eBay) in popularity, but they have a huge impact on the ability of businesses, and users in those businesses, to communicate with each other. Until now, communication within business has been slow and narrow. Needing to go through certain individuals to speak to one of your suppliers. Or potential suppliers not on your books never being able to communicate with you about what they sell. Which could be exactly what you need! Technology could open all this communication up.

Finally, trust in Procurement data, and indeed in all types of supply chain data, is set to be transformed by technology—specifically, blockchain. This is important because a significant portion of time today in Procurement is spent manually checking compliance in the supply chain, whether it is auditing suppliers, tracking and managing supplier performance, or paying for the goods and service they provide. Furthermore, who has ever been in a meeting looking at Procurement data and someone pipes up that they don't believe the data, or the data must be wrong? How about we rephrase that, who *hasn't* been in one of those meetings?

While blockchain is still to be properly let loose in the world of Procurement, it is coming, and its impact is going to be profound. Without going into the technicalities of it (not many people can!), blockchain is a secure method for tracking transactions that is not owned by any one person or system. The data is encrypted and cannot be changed without everyone in the chain being made aware. All of these characteristics (not owned by one person, encrypted, can't be changed) make the data in the chain completely trustworthy.

Investing in Technology—the Fundamentals

So, now that we can see the promised impact of technology in Procurement and we've learned about the potential perils of only investing in solutions without taking the wider operating model into account, how should you go about digitalizing the Procurement function? It's a question we get asked a lot and, as with many such questions, there is no one-size-fits-all answer.

For one, companies don't all have the same starting point. While some Procurement functions are still desperately manual, there are a few trail blazers out there who have been using technology to stream-line their operating models for years. And then there is everyone in between. There are, however, three common, guiding principles that most of the trail blazers have adhered to in order to ensure the success of their digitalization journey.

Own your data and don't over-configure!

I hosted a panel event at a Global Digital Procurement Summit last year, and one of the questions that was put to the panel was, "When considering Procurement technology, is it better to go for an end-to-end suite or adopt a best-of-breed approach of different tools?" I'd heard this question and debate many times before, and, in my opinion, both can work. But what is so much more important for a CPO is to own their data and then design their solution around that, whether it's end-to-end or best-of-breed.

The end-to-end versus best-of-breed debate becomes moot! Procurement functions suffer badly from a lack of data transparency: the source of most of their problems, in fact—be it not knowing how to prioritize work, struggling to find the most promising opportunities, not knowing how their suppliers are really performing, or rushing contract renewals a week before expiry. All these are caused by poor data. But it doesn't have to be this way. In fact, it is in the hands of the CPO to make sure it isn't!

So, you first need to create a plan and process for how you are going to take ownership of your data. A concrete example of this is simply linking spend and contract data. Having a common taxonomy for spend and contracts allows you to look at your contract coverage by category, which in turn enables you to know whether there could be a sourcing opportunity or indeed how much risk exposure you might be carrying in that category.

To make sure this is not just a one-off exercise, ensuring that spend data is live and new contracts are filed against the common taxonomy is key. Basic Procurement technology exists for this, and has done for years. But surprisingly few firms take care of this fundamental step. To advance this a little further, adding the same taxonomy to your list of Procurement initiatives, for example, (whether sourcing, supplier management, or otherwise) goes a long way. Every time an initiative is created, it should be assigned to a category from the same taxonomy, and the underlying spend data used to size the initiative should come from the same spend data set. Initiatives can also be assigned to owners from the team.

All of a sudden, we have a way of telling not only what our spend categories are, but also how many initiatives we have for each, the value of them, who is working on what, and whether there are contractual gaps. This enables much more effective prioritization and ensures that the team is working on the most value-adding things at any one time.

This is just a simple example of investing in master data management in a small area. But it can and must be expanded to other areas, such as supplier performance data, data from the P2P process, and more.

Having designed your future processes in a way that allows you to own your data, you are now ready to make your technology investment to help with their automation. And you will find many that can do the job. The key here is to find a solution that won't need a lot of configuring to fit your processes. A lot of money and time is spent unnecessarily configuring off-the-shelf technology to fit a very unique process that doesn't need to be very unique. If no technology exists without a serious configuration requirement, modify your future data process to fit.

Visualize your data

Getting on top of, and owning, your data is fundamental, as we have just seen. But to really harness the power of being on top of your data, you need to visualize it. There is some excellent data-visualization software out there that allows you to interpret and read what your Procurement data is telling you in a way that you could never do by looking at a raw data extract. Most people visualize their data in PowerPoint or Excel, if indeed they do it at all. But visualization software allows you to easily interrogate the data and drill down in a way you can't with a static PowerPoint graphic.

So, why is visualizing data important? Simply put, you are aiming to put data into the hands of decision makers. Decision makers who have, until now, made decisions on supplier awards, negotiations, work allocation, risk mitigation, and prioritizing, based purely on their feel for what is happening. This means more effective decisions and a revolution in how effective Procurement can be done as a result.

But, visualizing data is not just about buying software. That's the easy part. Understanding who needs to know what information to make them better at their job is the hard part. I have seen one company do this brilliantly, particularly in the area of supplier management. Its data and insights manager spent significant time talking to senior stakeholders to get an understanding of how they go about their role and the information that would help them manage certain suppliers better, if only they could get hold of it. The manager then worked back with her team to figure out how they could generate those insights and then what the data sources would be.

Needless to say, most of the data wasn't available immediately, so they set about putting in place processes to ensure the data would be built over time. That meant engaging suppliers for some of it. Some obliged, but not all it has to be said. But she wasn't afraid to draw a line in the sand, accept not being able to deliver the finished product straightaway, and then progress from there.

As data started coming in, she first presented the insights in the traditional static way: PowerPoint and Excel. The feedback was mixed. It turns out that translating what people say they want to see into something they actually want to see is not easy! So, she iterated. As her insights became more valuable with greater volumes of data, the company invested in a digitalization tool and a supplier communication tool to automate the collection of the data that had to come from suppliers. Other data from internal systems was also automated.

Because of the success of this initiative, all sourcing projects in the company are now required to ensure commitment from their chosen suppliers to provide relevant management information during the competitive tension part of the sourcing process, thus avoiding a potential repeat of the "unobliging supplier" syndrome mentioned earlier.

This iterative approach has led to a part-digitalization of this company's supplier management process. Data collection and analysis is now mostly automated, saving significant time. Granted, there is still a data validation step that requires human intervention, but it is manageable and over time the human requirement is decreasing.

But most importantly, people who make decisions on supplier management issues are now doing so in a data-driven, and by definition more effective, way because they can see the data they need in a digestible format.

Manage your knowledge

How many times do you think people spend reinventing the wheel when working on Procurement tasks? Well, I reckon you can double it. The classic example is Strategic Sourcing, in which contracts and categories need to be resourced every two to three years—or even multiple times in the same year, but by different regions or business units of the same global company.

Who can remember which suppliers we invited last year to the tender? What were our reward criteria? How did we ask the suppliers to price, and what cost model did we use? Given that you probably spent a lot of time figuring all that out from scratch the first time, isn't it surprising you didn't think to record it all and save yourself the trouble next time? Admittedly, you aren't necessarily going to run a carbon copy of the last sourcing process, but there will likely be many reusable elements. If only someone could hand them to you now, on a plate.

Those who used Microsoft Word in the late 1990s and early 2000s might remember that sweet, but occasionally annoying, animated paperclip that would suddenly appear in the bottom corner of the screen. "Clippy" was its nickname. "It looks like you're writing a letter," Clippy would say, correctly. "Would you like some help?" At this point, you could either boot Clippy into touch (which I sometimes did!), or click on "Yes, please." If you clicked "Yes, please," it would then give you a few suggested layout formats for your letter and other letter-writing tips—some more useful than others. The concept though, was excellent: helping someone to do something more effectively based on the past learnings of other people.

Procurement functions that want to digitalize should consider how they can help colleagues procure effectively by using their previous, and future, experience. Providing knowledge and guidance during some of the more complex processes—whether sourcing, supplier management, or otherwise—is an excellent start. This knowledge can take the form of templates, process guides, benchmarks, and more.

But the knowledge can't just be a dump of previous work or original files that might be useful. No one is going to use something that would take them longer to find than if they were just to do it themselves from scratch. It needs to be curated and useable content, it needs to be accessible, and it needs to be available when the person needs it. Taking the time to curate this content is an investment, but it will pay dividends down the line.

This is relevant for all businesses—in particular, for large global businesses for which this approach is an essential way to make good Procurement scalable in the organization.

So, when shopping for Procurement tools, make sure you have designed your knowledge management process first, and choose a solution that supports it. Interestingly, technology that supports Procurement processes and enables easy and effective knowledge management is less common today than you'd think. But in our view, it is critical; otherwise, you get a tool that might support your processes but does not allow you to scale them for the rest of the organization. It doesn't allow the rest of the organization to meet their own needs based on the intelligence you have built up and can provide to them.

Technological Disruption Is Coming!

Which leads us nicely to our concluding thoughts for the chapter. As we have discussed in the last few pages, business—and Procurement in particular—has been slow to adopt new technologies until now. But, make no mistake, if Procurement doesn't, another party will.

To put it bluntly, if Procurement doesn't leverage technology to move to another operating model soon, one which does not set itself up as a bottleneck, it will suffer the same fate as the travel agents we read about earlier, and find itself with a very limited role. The Procurement functions that survive will get out of the way for routine processes, allowing the business to easily serve itself.

Already, there are third parties targeting business users directly (bypassing Procurement). They offer pre-sourced deals for all sorts of products and services—user-friendly interfaces with the ability to consolidate payments, for example. Procurement needs to get there first and change its value proposition to the business. In this new operating model, Procurement seeks to add value by fine-tuning the machine: curating knowledge, spotting patterns, opportunities, and risk in the data, and allowing the business to easily buy what it needs at the best total cost.

This is the challenge technology poses to Procurement today. But it is also an incredible opportunity. With a focus on getting data and processes right first, and by considering the needs of the people in the business, Procurement can leverage technology to completely reposition itself for the better!

11

CONSULTANTS: Using Consultants in Procurement

OK, so let's get the consultant joke out of the way, shall we? Nothing like a bit of self-deprecation on behalf of your authors. Here's one of our favorites:

A man in a hot air balloon descends over a meadow where a shepherd is tending his flock.

After the balloonist greets the man, he asks him, "If I tell you how many sheep you have without having to count them, will you give me one of them?"

The shepherd agrees.

The man in the balloon says, "You have 100 sheep."

A bit surprised, the shepherd says, "How did you know?"

"Well," says the man, "your field is about 5 km by 5 km, and in this part of the wilderness you can graze four sheep on each square km of land. So, 5×5 is 25 square km × 4 is 100 sheep."

"Wow, you're right," said the shepherd, "please take your pick of my sheep!"

After the man in the balloon selects his sheep, the shepherd turns to him and says, "If I tell you what you do for a living, will you give me my animal back?"

The man in the balloon agrees. The shepherd says, "You are a consultant."

The man in the balloon is amazed at the insight that the shepherd has shown and says, "How on earth did you know I am a consultant?"

The shepherd answers, "You showed up here, fueled by nothing but hot air, even though nobody called you. You want to get paid for an answer I already knew, to a question I never asked. And you don't know a thing about my business ... now give me back my dog!"

Love the ending there. But on a more serious note, we (the authors) do believe an insider's perspective would be helpful on the topic of Procurement, given how many Procurement transformation programs involve sizeable consulting support.

So, let's talk about how best to select the right type of partner, how to best use them, how to make sure you get value from their engagement, and what to do when it all goes wrong.

Unfortunately, we can't give away any commercial secrets along the way ... we need to continue to work harmoniously with our colleagues!

Why Use Consultants?

There is an extremely wide spectrum from "good use of consultants" to "terrible use of consultants," and we've all heard of examples of the latter ... it really can go very wrong. But particularly, when it comes to Procurement, consultants can add—and accelerate—a huge amount of value. They just have to be used in the right way ... using the right people to do the right job in the right way, while working effectively with your people in an integrated manner.

Our first example of a good use of Procurement consultants is in the "Opportunity Assessment" or "30-Day Plan" phase—to shape and size the program. Consultants are very good at some things and not very good at others. What they are very good at is quickly and accurately sizing and segmenting your spend, interviewing the organization to unearth the opportunities, and backing that up with compelling evidence and a clear plan for moving forward.

It's analytical, it involves large volumes of (spend) data, it's "outside looking in," and the result is a structured plan. This is where consultants excel. What would take your people six months, good consultants can do in one, because they have the luxury of being able to focus on the task 100% without distraction. Plus, it's the first piece of work, so you can use it to test them and get to know them on a short analytical piece of work before you commit to something bigger.

This short analytical piece also gives them all the facts they need to provide you with a clear proposal to help with the execution. It also provides the consultants with the insights needed before embarking on any type of "fee at risk" commercial arrangement. So, using consultants for the initial, short, sharp diagnostic, makes eminent sense.

The second effective use of Procurement consultants lies in the area of sourcing execution, because it plays to the consultants' skill set. Sourcing requires the analytical, numeracy, communication, and influencing skills that consultants tend to have in abundance, and it requires large amounts of motivation and tenacity. Consultants just make for great interim or project-based sourcing execution resources; in many ways, they have exactly the skills that you wish your buyers had (I can't count the number of times CPOs have told me, "I wish I had people like yours.").

The other reason for using consultants for sourcing and savings delivery has to do with timing. In a situation where you're transforming your Procurement team, there is some lag time due to ramp-up. It will take the CPO at least a year to get his new, high-performing team in place. Why do nothing during that year, when you could use consultants to start attacking the categories and generating savings? So, use the consultants to plug your resource gaps until your team is in place. In fact, most of the Procurement transformation consulting programs I've sold have essentially had the dual objective of (i) delivering significant savings, *while* (ii) building up the long-term capability … but doing them in parallel, rather than sequentially, which would involve losing a year.

Consultants are also a good way to "variabilize" your cost base. Procurement has peaks and troughs when it comes to resource requirements, so why not staff up permanently to the base load, then use consultants as and when required to top up. The biggest peak in Procurement activity occurs during the sourcing phase; once the spend is sourced, there is a much lower need for permanent Procurement resources. Another reason to use consultants early then—have them help you get through the sourcing activity for the first 18 months, then pull things back to a smaller in-house team.

A final area where it makes sense to bring in consultants is, of course, the whole topic of Procurement IT systems implementation. Here you need help with program management, process mapping, process design, platform customization, and implementation. These can be large consulting programs with significant over-runs in terms of both time and cost, and care must be taken around the promised benefits. The latter will be in the form of process efficiencies, which are comparatively small and difficult to bank; and in the form of compliance benefits; i.e., a mechanism to ensure that the spend flows to your chosen suppliers, who are assumed to have more attractive pricing. That will be true, but only after you've sourced your spend ... the P2P system is an *enabler* of benefit, but it doesn't bring the benefit per se. Our advice when it comes to a P2P implementation project is, make sure you speak to a range of providers and experts, to build up a full picture of the potential pitfalls and the various available ways of avoiding them.

There is one final point regarding when to use consultants, and this concerns the skillsets that you're buying from them. I've spent 25 years pitching Procurement consulting programs. Over that period, by far the most common challenge or objection I've received has consistently been around category experience—to the point where it seems that many of our clients engaged us primarily because of our category experience. It would seem to be the most important criterion when choosing a Procurement consultant. And yet ... looking at it from the other side, as a consultant who has spent a quarter of a century helping clients to source complex categories ... it's actually not *that* important.

Sure, categories like IT and manufactured components, in particular, require subject matter expertise; but for most categories, other considerations are more important. In fact, when I'm looking to staff my teams, category knowledge comes very low on my list of priorities.

There are a number of reasons for this: (i) it's actually fairly easy to learn about a supply market and a category ... it's an easy skills gap to plug; (ii) you, the client, already *have* the buyer who's been buying mid-range transformers (or whatever it may be) for 27 years; he / she will work with the consultant hand in hand ... the deep supply market expertise can come from the client side—it's already there; (iii) often it's actually helpful to not know your category too well ... it opens up new lines of questioning, whereas decades of experience can make one blinkered; and (iv) dealing with the suppliers is the *easy* part, because you have power/leverage over them. They will comply in the end, most likely, but the internal stakeholders may not ... the bigger challenge lies in managing the change internally, which does not require category expertise.

The skills deficit that you have in Procurement is likely *not* around category knowledge ... what you're more likely lacking is analytical horsepower, hard workers that go the extra mile, and those all-important influencing and communication skills. You'd be better served to probe those skills during the consultants' pitches ... because that's where you need the help. So, rather than asking how many times a firm has sourced a certain category, try to understand in detail how their people speak to their experience in overcoming issues like lack of data and lack of business buy-in. That said, category experience *is* important, but it's a little more nuanced than that.

How to Select the Right Consulting Partner

Which leads us neatly to our next topic—how to select the right partner. Clearly, when it comes to consultants, there is a very wide spectrum of firms and individuals from which to choose—in terms of type of support, type / size of firm, geographic footprint, and price point. Let's take a quick look at the three main groups of Procurement consultants: the large global firms, the smaller specialist firms, and the contractor market.

All the big firms—the strategy houses like McKinsey, BCG, and others, and the audit-based firms like PwC and Deloitte—have a Procurement offering and would be keen to take your money. The big firms have very broad capabilities and a huge amount of expertise. They also have powerful brands, and it's no doubt easier to sell your Procurement strategy to your Board, if said strategy is endorsed by McKinsey. These firms are also almost all truly global in nature—an important consideration in cross-border Procurement. They typically have very strong executive-level relationships with their clients, which they leverage to get things done in the organization. They're credible, they're glossy, and this can really help to bring an organization together around a shared goal. And finally, the global firms have very large industry practices—so, if your purchases are very industry-specific (such as chemicals, for example), then this industry knowledge can be very helpful.

In 25 years pitching Procurement projects in competition with the global firms, your authors have had plenty of success—but when we did lose against the large firms, it was for one of three reasons only: (i) greater geographic presence, (ii) better strategic level industry insight, and (iii) pre-existing relationships—the large firms are often already well positioned with many clients. The "minuses" of the larger firms are: (i) depth of expertise in Procurement, which varies significantly across the larger firms, and (ii) price—the day rates of the global firms, particularly the strategy houses, are still very expensive, and companies with revenues below $300 or $400m struggle to make the economics work ... their spend is not big enough to yield a strong return on investment from engaging these firms.

Next up are the specialist Procurement consulting firms. There has been a trend towards using functional experts in consulting for the last 25 or so years, and the Procurement specialist firms have been growing at pace. Particularly the Private Equity houses, which work extensively with the strategy firms during due diligence and acquisition, often prefer to use experts in areas like Procurement and pricing, where subject matter expertise is important.

However, the specialist firms don't necessarily come with a brand you know you can rely on. They're smaller and less well known, and you have to know the players to understand their relative quality levels, which can vary widely. The quality of the people is also much more variable—the big firms have a set formula for how, and from where, to recruit and grow their people, and the quality level is very homogenous. The smaller firms tend to be a more diverse collection of individuals from different backgrounds, so there tends to be less consistency and uniformity. There can also be a somewhat formulaic / "sausage machine" approach that does not lend itself well to the more strategic and complex categories, which is why most specialist firms focus on indirect Procurement.

The big plus of the specialist firms, on the other hand, is that they often have more subject-matter expertise. Where the big firms are sometimes accused of being too generalist, the key advantage of the specialists is that they're focused on what they do, and they know their stuff.

And it's less about the category experience, as we said before—it's more about the *sourcing* experience. Experience in where to obtain the data to build the baseline, ability to build a complex dynamic bid analysis tool, and experience in pulling together a supplier RFP launch meeting that makes the suppliers take the exercise seriously.

Relevant execution skills ... knowing what to do to start collecting data, knowing upfront what *types* of sourcing strategies are worth considering. If you can find a niche firm that combines this hands-on expertise with strategic thinking and very strong individuals, then you can quickly find yourself in territory where the specialist firm could be more effective. Having said that, we would recommend that you probe their mix of experience across direct and indirect spend—there are many "indirects houses" that are not fit-for-purpose for strategically sourcing complex direct materials.

The second fundamental reason to think about a specialist firm is cost and ROI. The niche firms have much lower day rates than the premium generalist firms: their rates are less than half of those of the global firms, and often even lower. And then there's ROI—large multi-national companies, with spends in the billions of dollars, can achieve an excellent ROI from using a premium firm, whereas, say, a mid-cap company with only $150m of Procurement spend will find the fees exorbitant in relation to the savings, and is effectively priced out of the premium firm market by the small magnitude of its spend. This is leading the niche firms to target the mid-market that can't afford the large firms ... which, in turn, has spurred the growth and development of the niche firms over the last 20 years. The large consulting houses are impressive organizations with highly talented people and very deep client relationships. In the last 20 years, they have been joined by a small number of high-caliber specialists that warrant serious consideration.

One deciding factor between generalist and niche may be your geographic footprint. If you're a global or even multi-national organization, you will struggle to find many specialist firms that can match your footprint in terms of their office locations or their ability to deploy. That's because most smaller firms struggle to develop beyond their original market. There are a number of German firms, British firms, and US firms, but many of them don't reach beyond their own borders, which is clearly a limiting factor in the world of Procurement. Growing a consulting firm beyond 100 people is very difficult, so that's another indicator—size as a proxy for success.

The third option, when looking for external help, is the contractor market—in other words, individual contractors / sole traders. These resources are considerably cheaper than even the niche firms and often come loaded with many years of Procurement experience. I have seen many clients turn to the contractor route when faced with multi-million-dollar consulting engagements. However, we believe firmly that this is a false economy. The quality is highly variable in the contractor market and is not in any way pre-vetted; individual contractors may or may not have proper consulting skills; they typically move at a slower pace than consulting firms; and there is a risk that they become quasi-employees that are difficult to "turn off."

The biggest drawback is that you're now managing a group of disparate individuals who don't even know each other, rather than managing a professional firm. It can take months or even years to get people to play from the same playbook; and with a consultancy, consistency of approach is core. Our recommendation: use contractors to plug gaps in your team, but don't use them in lieu of a consulting firm in the mistaken belief that you're getting something similar for a lower price—you're not.

Buying a cohesive team is something very different to buying a group of separate individuals. The saving from using contractors is not there when you look on a "TCO basis;" you will find that a group of contractors will likely not achieve the same result as a consulting firm. They're fundamentally not the same thing, period. That's why the price is so much lower.

How do you choose the right firm? Consulting firms can be very difficult to select, because there is no tangible product to look at. Invite five of them in to give a PowerPoint presentation on their approach to Procurement, and their chevron charts all look much the same.

Also, what you get in the pitch room is not the product you're buying, day-to-day. That partner may be a brilliant presenter and salesman, but he / she is not the one who will be working in your organization. So, make sure you vet the individual people.

And here again, you don't always need category experience. "Gray-haired experts" who have 25 years of experience sourcing bearings ... these end-of-careerers are not the droids you're looking for if you want to make transformational change and a massive impact on your company's profitability. But equally, if no-one on the team is older than 25, you might have a problem.

Once you know which firm you want to work with, make sure you get a commitment to get their best people, their A team. Every firm has an A, B, and C team, so reach for the cream, and be sure to do this *during* the competitive selection process, while you still have leverage.

How Should I Best Use the Consultants?

Just a few thoughts on this question. (Obvious) point number one: use the consultants on the high impact stuff. We've been invited to tender on Procurement consulting projects looking at "the tail spend" many, many times. It's a model whereby the client addresses the strategic categories and suppliers with their internal team and uses consultants to manage "B spend" and "C spend."

Now, if you have a world-class team, then that makes sense. But when you have a "stone age" Procurement team, why have your $60k buyer manage the strategic categories and have your $3,000 to $5,000 a day consultant look after the tail of small suppliers, which is hugely effort-intensive for very little return. It will go down well with your internal team ... but it doesn't make any sense.

The answer is, of course, to team the consultants up with your best people and have them address the strategic categories together. Don't bring in consultants and then work to minimize their scope. It's not a good approach!

Beyond that, as we said before, the skillset of consultants matches well with Strategic Sourcing: a mix of analytical, commercial, people, and communication skills is what works, and good consultants tend to have these. So, have the consultants do the sourcing, either doubling up with your buyers, while your buyer dedicates only 15–20% of their time to the project, but the consultant supports him or her full-time by driving the data gathering, doing the analytics, and preparing the discussion documents needed to get people on board; or, if your team is not yet fully in place, let the consultants drive some categories while you drive the others.

By deploying consultants on sourcing execution roles, you're making sure that their deliverable is a new supplier contract, rather than a stack of PowerPoint slides. Using highly talented consultants in a purely advisory capacity is a waste—get them to deliver savings, not reports!

How Do I Make Sure That I Get the Best Value from My Consultants?

That's a slightly different question to "How should I best use them?" How do you make sure you get best value from your consultants? The short answer is that it's all about the long-term sustainability of what they deliver.

So much good consulting work goes nowhere, and it has nothing to do with the quality of the advice. The reason for lack of impact from a consulting program is most likely that what was done was not transferred to your people, so it died out when the consultants left. And that's the big risk with any consulting program—will it have any impact, or will it be another shelved report?

So, Rule Number One is to integrate the consultants with your best people. Or, if you don't have any best people yet, borrow some from Finance or elsewhere. You need to be sure that by the time the consultant involved in that Energy sourcing project packs his bags, your Energy buyer has a full understanding of the sourcing process, the reasons we chose the chosen suppliers, the agreed volumes, and pricing, the terms of the contract, etc. That's a lot of detail, so be sure your people are at least shadowing the consultants wherever possible.

In an ideal world, you would have planned your sourcing program so that the Bearings sourcing project lead becomes the Bearings category buyer at the end of the process. That way, there is continuity in the role, and the loss of the consultant is much more manageable.

The second rule is, make sure they leave something behind. At a bare minimum, of course, make sure they hand over working files, spreadsheets, and what have you. But beyond that, these days consultants come equipped with analysis tools, templates, even technologies (spend analytics, e-sourcing, contract management, …)—good sourcing consultants will leave their category with an ordering system, a savings tracking process and tool, and an ongoing supplier review, and management process in place. The more of the consultant's output can be enshrined in a simple technology tool, the more chance that it will be applied going forward. So, make sure to ask your consultants, "What are you going to leave behind for me?"

Third, do not allow an atmosphere of "us and them" to develop between your people and the consultants. It is completely normal and to-be-expected that your people will feel threatened and defensive when the consultants first come through the door. Personally I've found most client leaders struggle to deal with consultant versus employee issues. For some, the solution is to focus their own people on some parts of the program, while having the consultants take care of others. But this effectively then delineates and splits their roles and targets, which is a no-no. Join the targets up, "one team, one baseline, one saving," otherwise you'll spend half your time arguing over who gets credit for what.

In a similar vein, risk–reward / savings-based commercial arrangements can make things worse if they are not properly thought through. They can drive the wrong behaviors in your people and in the consultants, and if the targets are divisive, they will again drive an "us and them" dynamic.

This chapter does not offer advice on the consultants' pricing, but we will say that risk-reward commercials can be very workable and powerful if set up in the right way. Unfortunately, we've seen more unbalanced models than balanced ones—a balanced model being one where the consultant assumes a *reasonable* amount of risk in return for a *fair* reward. It is human nature to push these things too far, and unequitable risk-reward arrangements are very common.

If you do enter into such an arrangement, make sure that you don't make the mistake of not thinking about the fees until project end. It is essential to manage the fee discussion from Day One: be clear on the targets, monitor the savings progression, and agree on the principles of how to agree on savings in each category—ideally at the time of establishing the baseline. The more you work on this throughout, the less surprises, mismatched expectations, and arguments you can expect at the end.

It's All About the People

Ultimately, of course, consulting is all about people.

As mentioned before, Job One is to make sure that you're getting the consultancy's best people, their "A team." This can only really be done at the beginning, and you should use the competitive tension of the selection process to push for the firm's best resources.

It's also in your interest to make sure you get enough time and attention from the partner—the more time he or she spends on the job, the better his or her people should perform. Plus, you'll want to use the partner as a sounding board and a confidant. During the first three or four weeks of the program, a pattern of partner visit frequency will naturally emerge; if you're demanding during these weeks, the pattern will be one of frequent visits; if you're not, it won't.

As with all team endeavors, constant communication and feedback are of the upmost importance. Over the years I've had a few clients who had an approach of "give the consultants a damn good kicking every few weeks, to avoid them becoming complacent." Well, it was not pleasant, I can say that ... but it sure did work.

As a client, when you shout at the consultants or complain to them, you get their attention. To a professional services firm, the client is sacrosanct, and what the client says, goes. So, make sure you're being heard ... at all times, and loud and clear. Of course, a good kicking is only effective if there's sometimes also a hug. Like all humans, consultants just want a bit of recognition ... or should I say, as insecure over-achievers, they crave recognition a lot more than most people. The more junior people, in particular, will hugely appreciate even a small piece of positive client feedback, and this will no doubt give a boost to their motivation and performance.

Back to the other extreme ... if you really can't get along with one of the consultants, then say so, and insist on a replacement. I remember launching a big sourcing transformation program with a client in the

UK, where we deployed over 20 consultants, which is a big team. Once my team had been onboarded, the client came to me to explain that he loved 18 of the 20, but two of them didn't fit and had to be switched out. My reaction was that the client was well within his rights to insist on this, and it didn't really cost me anything, just a call to our Staffing team to make a swap.

Weaning Yourself Off the Drug

It has been said that consulting is like a drug, that once you make your first buy, you'll end up dependent on them, and unable to get them back out (that is, assuming the collaboration was a success!).

Certainly, a client who buys a consulting project receives an injection of talent, momentum, and horsepower, and it's easy to become dependent on your consultants. They're high-caliber people, they work around the clock, and they do what you ask—sometimes more willingly, quickly, and effectively than your own team. So, what to do to avoid dependence?

The answer is, to continue the drug analogy, most definitely not to terminate the consultants "cold turkey"—it would put the body in shock, unable to cope with the sudden blanket withdrawal. Much better to wean yourself off over time. In the world of sourcing, that's particularly pertinent. You're likely embarking on an 18- to 24-month program divided into three or four sourcing waves; and you're slowly onboarding and educating your own team.

So ... use the consultants heavily in the initial waves of sourcing, to show your team the way, and then gradually, over subsequent waves of sourcing, have your team take up the reins and learn to become self-sufficient. I've personally sold many Procurement transformation programs on this "weaning off" basis—**Figure 11.1** illustrates the concept.

If you read the detail in Figure 11.1, you will see that significant efforts were made to enable and smooth the transition from consultant-led to client-led. The sourcing process was not only used by the teams, it was fully embedded across the organization; supporting tools and technologies were put in place; and a multi-module Strategic Sourcing training program was rolled out to all Procurement staff

Weaning Yourself Off the Consultants–Client Example

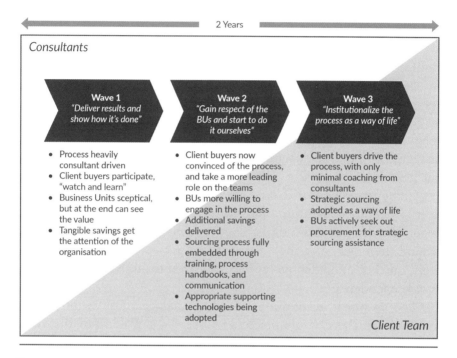

Figure 11.1   Weaning Yourself Off the Consultants—Client Example

globally. And it worked! It wasn't perfect … it was still not easy for the client to lose the support of the consultants. But the program continued, and the savings kept rolling in, long after the consultants were gone.

It was one of the most successful programs of my career, and key to it was the concept of "in Wave I, we'll take the lead and show you what to do; in Wave II, we will hold your hand … ; and in Wave III, we'll set you free." The best part about it is that the client started with very little skill or credibility residing in their Procurement function.

So, in Wave I, we consultants were indeed the teachers, and we were literally building up the client's capability from scratch. But we were also delivering massive savings to the business: so, rather than asking the broader client organization to *invest* in Procurement for

12 months while we built up the capability ... we gave them *savings* after only six months. And, of course, the savings then helped boost the credibility and the confidence of the Procurement team further, and the whole thing became a virtuous cycle.

Conclusion: plan for the end of the consultants proactively from Day One and set out a gradual shift of ownership from the consultants to your team. But be under no illusion: once the consultants leave, it will be more difficult to keep up the drumbeat, it will be harder to push the business, and it will be harder to get the work done. Make sure your team really is ready to pick up the reins.

What Do We Do When It All Goes Horribly Wrong ... or How to Avoid That Happening

It's beyond the remit of this book to go into detail about how to effectively run a consulting program. But it's worth giving just a little thought to the nightmare scenario, of which there are many real-life examples, of your project spinning out of control and you having to throw good money after bad in an effort to turn it around.

The most infamous consulting screw-ups are scenarios in which a bad situation was allowed to continue without an effective rescue intervention. I have one client who ended up spending $1 billion implementing an ERP system across the U.K. and the U.S. And this is a non-manufacturing company!

The good news about sourcing projects is that they can usually be turned around. The key is to spot the problem, call a time out, re-tool, and go again.

I've had several projects in my career that have run into major problems, where the client has called me and said he / she was not happy. Upon examination, the sourcing teams were spinning, the business was not engaged, things were a mess.

In my experience, the key in these situations is to create an intervention. Admit that there is a major problem (and nobody wants to admit that to their boss, and the consultant certainly doesn't want to admit it to the client). Admit that there is a problem, create a detailed and formal "get out of the s***" plan, make some visible people changes (usually that's the problem anyway), and then mount a massive project rescue effort. Unfortunately, human nature is often to take the very opposite approach—minimize the problem, keep everyone happy, don't rock the boat, kick the can down the road.

Of course, the real answer is to not allow things to reach that point in the first place. And that's down to good program management. Most important of all is proper governance and full and active stakeholder engagement. If the CFO never shows up to the Steering Committee, and the head of the largest business unit sends her assistant, you're going nowhere. In my experience, there is a direct correlation between the success of a project and the degree and consistency of C-level engagement. When there is great C-level engagement, half the battle is won.

Beyond this, a successful project needs a central drumbeat that drives it forward relentlessly, which usually takes the form of a Program Office. That Office has to avoid being a bureaucratic burden, but instead create a cascade of diarized calls and meetings that drive the program forward. This includes weekly sourcing team meetings, weekly sourcing team PMO update calls, weekly leadership update calls, and monthly Steering Committees. It's a sausage machine that needs to work seamlessly.

For a large sourcing program, you should have a two-person PMO: the consultancy's day-to-day program manager, typically Senior Engagement Manager or Principal level, working full time; and your own overall program manager. This is the most critical appointment of your Procurement transformation.

Your program manager sits at the heart of the program, managing the whole suite of stakeholders involved. His or her job is to constantly remove blockages that occur within each sourcing team. The stakeholder refuses to give them their data, the data doesn't exist, France and Italy have not replied to any of the information requests, the Engineering Director is planning a parallel initiative to look at his supply base, the Marketing supplier has contacted the Marketing Director directly in an effort to undermine the bid process. Your PMO person needs to get all of these small obstacles cleared. So, he / she needs to be very well connected in the organization, liked by his / her peers, respected by senior management, not afraid to speak his / her mind, and, above all, tenacious.

Proper governance and senior stakeholder involvement then, along with a structured PMO that includes a strong lead from the client side, are key to avoiding project meltdown in the first place.

Coming back to the consultant joke at the start of this chapter—so, is Procurement consulting really just a lot of hot air? The answer is, of course, it is what you make it.

Procurement consulting is like Procurement technology, in that you can't just buy it and expect to thereby fix everything; you have to deploy it in the right way, you have to combine it appropriately with your existing resources, and you have to make sure you get a quantifiable and healthy return on your investment.

Hopefully this chapter has provided some useful thinking around why, when, and where you might engage consultants, how to select the right ones and, once selected, how best to work with them so that you yield maximum value from the project.

If you get it right, the use of consultants can be a fantastic launch-pad for a Procurement transformation program. It makes sense to use them early in the journey, while your people are not yet in place, to drive savings and to "show the way" to your people. Just make sure you have a plan for "weaning yourself off"—like overcoming a drug addiction, take the drug away carefully over time, by having your people assume more and more of the "driving" over the life of the program.

And talking of people … make sure you put your best people on the project, working hand-in-glove with the consultants. That way, they absorb the knowledge of the consultants along the way, and there won't be any issues when it comes to saying good-bye.

12

PRIVATE EQUITY: Learning Lessons from PE

You may wonder why this book has a whole chapter devoted to Private Equity, when it's only relevant to a subset of our audience. This book's authors have worked extensively with the world's leading PE firms to drive Procurement benefits, and we've seen over and over again that Procurement and PE can be a powerful combination. Private Equity is very interested in the relatively painless potential to generate savings that drop straight to the bottom line, and the more sophisticated firms are highly proactive in creating a platform that permits Procurement to step up and deliver. There are interesting lessons for all of us in this, and that is what this chapter will explore.

Of course, our intent here is not to encourage you to sell your company to Private Equity! And it's also not to promote the "PE model" over other ownership models. It is merely to hold up Private Equity as an interesting example of what can be achieved in Procurement when there is a high level of interest in the function, and when a platform is created for it to step up and deliver cross-functionally.

We've talked extensively about how Procurement is under-invested in many companies because the "top table" fails to recognize its potential. The more progressive PE firms *do* recognize that potential and *are* willing to make that investment. The mid-cap companies that PE tends to buy often have quite basic Procurement functions at best ... and yet in the space of a couple of years, these firms often manage to put the function on the map and successfully drive significant profit uplift through Procurement.

This chapter explores Private Equity and Procurement as a case study—with the conclusion that there isn't necessarily a PE magic sauce, but rather that, given the right level of interest, investment, and support, Procurement can flourish and make a huge impact on profitability and, ultimately, company value. If we can replicate this same level of interest, support, and investment in the function, then half the battle is already won. In essence, this chapter is a case study in creating the right platform. We believe this is an absolutely critical success factor in transforming Procurement, and that we can learn powerful (but ultimately simple) lessons from PE in this regard.

Private Equity and Procurement

Private Equity is a vehicle for shareholder value creation. And value, or a company's value, is typically measured using a multiple of EBITDA. An Opex Procurement saving that drops straight to the bottom line then, could be worth 10 times its value in the eyes of an investor looking to sell the company in the medium term. This is good news for Procurement.

Of course, good PE funds also have an equally important objective of building a sustainable company for the long term. But there's no denying that a Private Equity owner will take a keen interest in anything that moves the EBITDA needle. In fact, Procurement is often where PE starts when it comes to cost management ... it's the "easy win," involving no headcount reduction, plant closures, or risky investments. The fact that most mid-market companies (the companies that PE tends to buy) have under-performing Procurement functions, and often no function at all, makes it doubly attractive. It means that there is significant low-hanging fruit to be harvested, helping PE in its objective of making an early impact on the companies it buys.

As one would expect, there is a wide spectrum of PE companies, and their modus operandi vary greatly. The small cap PE houses that invest in smaller, founder-led businesses (such as Efficio, the authors' employer) tend to interfere very little with their companies operationally. The large cap PE houses (think KKR, Bain Capital, Blackstone, the Carlyle Group) are much more operationally involved in their portfolios. Across the large cap firms, styles also vary greatly, from almost completely hands off to extremely hands on, depending on the firm's philosophy, size, and resources.

But what we've seen again and again is that when a PE owner embraces Procurement as part of the value creation process, it creates a unique opportunity and platform for Procurement to step up and be counted. And when Procurement does rise to that challenge, the PE parent can be a fantastic ally *during* the Procurement journey. This chapter explores what it is that works well in the PE environment—and tries to distil potential learnings for the rest of us.

Changing Attitudes

PE's attitude to Procurement, and to cost reduction in general, has changed a lot in the last 10–12 years. Since the 2008 financial crisis, we've seen significantly more focus on cost than on growth, and the PE firms are starting to realize that focusing on *both* is in fact possible and necessary. As a result, many of the large PE firms have invested in bigger and bigger "ops teams"—groups of highly charged ex-strategy consultants and / or executives whose role it is to effect operational improvements in their companies.

These days, the large cap PE houses typically kick things off as soon as the ink on the deal is dry, with an ambitious Value Creation Plan (VCP) that includes both growth and cost management initiatives. The degree to which Procurement is part of this plan varies. The more progressive firms have realized that Procurement can be a quick, painless, and almost guaranteed EBITDA enhancer … The Procurement leg of the VCP will deliver hard savings after six months, whereas the other workstreams can take much longer; Procurement, then, buys you time and funds the rest of the VCP.

It also happens to address 50–80% of the cost base, which can't be a bad thing.

So, Procurement is squarely on the map for the more progressive large cap PE funds. Let's look at what that means in practice, and why it matters.

So Why Are Procurement and PE Such a Good Match?

Two reasons. One, Private Equity has embraced Procurement as a significant EBITDA lever and will create a platform for the function to deliver; and two, organizationally, the PE owner is in a fantastic position to help expedite the delivery of results.

More specifically, a Private Equity owner can help to maximize Procurement benefits for six key reasons:

1. PE is all about value creation and EBITDA—a great fit with Procurement.
2. PE "gets" the Procurement opportunity and creates a platform to deliver the potential.
3. PE helps with speed and rigor of execution.
4. Joint ownership creates the right incentives and behaviors.
5. PE elevates Procurement to executive level, which facilitates cross-functionality.
6. Leading PE funds drive Procurement as a structured program across their portfolios.

Let's examine each of these in turn.

1) PE is all about value creation and EBITDA, a great fit with Procurement

As already noted, Private Equity cares deeply about improving EBITDA, and Procurement—which influences 50–80% of a company's costs—is a huge underexploited lever in accomplishing this, as discussed in Chapter 1: Introduction. Put simply, for PE, a $1 saving equates to a $10 increase in equity valuation (assuming a 10-fold profit multiple), which makes its focus on EBITDA razor-sharp. Most companies are focused on their profitability, regardless of the ownership setup. PE is just *more* focused on it, and that makes a huge difference. And that focus goes beyond the generation of the operational saving, but encompasses compliance, savings realization, and impact on budgets—all of which are helpful to Procurement.

2) PE "gets" the Procurement opportunity and creates a platform to deliver the potential

In Chapter 1, we talked about the fact that many companies' executive teams simply don't appreciate the opportunity inherent in Procurement. Private Equity (or at least, the more sophisticated firms) just "gets" the Procurement opportunity. It has fully internalized the fact that effecting a profit impact through Procurement is in many respects easier and *quicker* than competing improvement initiatives.

PE also likes to take a "no stones unturned" approach to the external spend. Some of the larger houses have teams that create and administer cross-portfolio deals in indirect spend categories such as Office Supplies, Car Rental, Laptops, etc. Others prefer an approach of working company-by-company, looking at the much larger but company-specific direct materials. In both cases, PE will be an advocate of looking at all the options and exercising all possible levers, which is of course good for Procurement.

What's also good for Procurement is that Private Equity people are investors at heart, and if you show them that you can deliver significant Procurement savings, then they will likely sanction the required investment in your function … because the ROI is likely to be at least five-fold. For the CPO of the portfolio company, this is his / her chance to finally get that mandate, and to finally unlock the investment required in the function. The economics of driving a Procurement program are obvious … but somebody needs to listen, understand, and decide to go for it. PE is often that somebody.

3) PE helps with speed and rigor of execution

There is more good news once the investment case is signed off and the Procurement transformation is underway. Good PE companies (or at least PE companies with good ops teams) excel at execution. They devise ambitious 100-day plans and set up a focused VCP, which they then execute in a highly disciplined manner.

In Chapter 3: Sourcing Execution, we discussed the myriad of roadblocks that sourcing teams invariably encounter along their journey, and the need to remove these roadblocks quickly and effectively to allow the teams to succeed. PE firms are in a strong position to help with this. The biggest roadblock of all is when spend is deemed un-addressable; in other words, considered out-of-bounds. This phenomenon often affects 30–50% of the external spend, due to supplier relationships, over-engineered specs that prevent you from accessing a wider market, or non-compliance to group deals by autonomous business units. PE can help alleviate these blockages, thus making more of the spend available and accelerating the path to savings.

Ultimately, PE investors are agents of change. They are almost allergic to the status quo and will work relentlessly to slay sacred cows and to not let personal agendas roadblock the value creation process. Procurement needs to seize this opportunity to ride on the coattails of PE's ambition, momentum, and drive.

4) Joint ownership creates the right incentives and behaviors

Private Equity firms are the (often majority-) owner of their companies, and they've invested in order to grow the EBITDA and then cash out and make a return on their money. Therefore, their incentives are clear, and they're driven towards a pre-planned exit timeline of around five years.

More importantly, the sale of a company to PE usually involves Management also being given significant and clear incentives based on EBITDA performance. Through its incentivization based on EBITDA, PE manages to make Procurement important to Management, which was previously not the case. The end result is that there is often a sharp focus on Procurement, from the owner down to senior management, and there is an expectation that the function can help them achieve their objectives.

5) PE elevates Procurement to Executive Committee level, which facilitates cross-functionality

In Chapter 6: Cross-Functional Change, and throughout this book, we've talked about the importance of engaging cross-functionally, and about the need for the C-Suite to take an active interest and to lubricate the cross-functional wheels. The PE company is represented on the Board and has influence over the top team and the Value Creation Plan. This usually elevates Procurement on to the radar of the Executive Committee, and this in turn has an enormous unlocking effect, because the committee is cross-functional (or non-functional?) by definition. It can make instant decisions that might otherwise get mired in cross-functional debate. And it makes Procurement an Executive Committee issue, rather than a back office one. It also makes the function a strategic partner with the other leaders in the organization.

More than this, at executive level, PE has the unique power to intervene *across functions* in the portfolio company. Ops group executives often act as a cross-functional glue. The PE firm's representative on the company's Board is typically quite vocal. He or she will be an important sponsor of Procurement as part of the VCP, and (depending on the individual) a possibly powerful force in pushing for the right thing.

I have sat in countless Executive Committee meetings where nobody would outright challenge or disagree with the CEO or CFO … but the PE partner did! So, when in normal companies, the decision just doesn't get made, or the conflict just doesn't get acknowledged, and the status quo wins … in a PE environment, an uncomfortable change (such as a direct materials supplier change) is more likely to be pushed through based on its merits.

Of course, the fact that PE is private also means that it's more willing to make big moves and invest in change, without the constraints of the quarterly performance pressures faced by public companies.

PE focuses heavily on areas like talent, Procurement, and FP&A as a matter of course, and Procurement benefits from this.

At the end of the day, Procurement and Private Equity are just a very good match—Procurement can influence 50% plus of all costs and can drive large EBITDA gains, with a great ROI; and Private Equity can help Procurement to push through the change. A match made in heaven if ever I saw one!

But, while PE acts as a great catalyst and "jumping off point" for big change, it's down to the CPO to harness this … and to balance medium-term savings delivery with building a long-term sustainable function. PE is often accused of being short-term focused. However, I'm finding that the more sophisticated PE houses have fully internalized the need for a sustainable ongoing capability in Procurement.

A CPO client of mine was recently pitching his Procurement transformation plan to the company Executive Committee; the PE partner was pleased about the massive savings delivered in the first two years of the transformation but was even more interested in what the Procurement function would be able to deliver "steady state" in four or five years' time …. He wanted to use the newly gained Procurement capability as a differentiator for a future buyer.

6) Leading PE funds drive Procurement as a structured program across their portfolios

As already mentioned, the degree of proactivity around cost reduction in general, and around Procurement in particular, varies significantly from PE fund to PE fund. The most sophisticated firms work hard to drive Procurement across their entire portfolios, regardless of industry or size of company spend, and they drive it in the form of a structured program. We've talked about the importance of doing this in other chapters, and the better PE firms serve as a powerful example of this.

By way of a case study, one leading U.S. firm with whom we've worked extensively considers Procurement to be a "bread and butter" issue—a must-have capability akin to talent management and financial forecasting and planning. They drive a structured four-pronged Procurement program, which involves (i) effecting an immediate one-time step-down in spend in the first 12 to 18 months, often with the help of external consultants; (ii) "lifting" the function to Executive Committee level and fundamentally improving the function's capability; (iii) heavily engaging with Finance to ensure savings validation and effective budgeting; and (iv) managing the spend on an ongoing basis to drive savings year-on-year. This approach is followed at every portfolio company, thus making sure that Procurement is always a priority, while at the same time balancing short- to medium-term savings with long-term capability and sustainability.

This Private Equity fund has fully recognized the importance of involving Finance and puts a relentless focus on tracking savings to the bottom line. The issue of savings tracking and realization is a complex one, as discussed in Chapter 5: Operating Model. What's interesting to note with regards to PE is that, despite these firms' financial sophistication, savings realization is still their number one unsolved issue. But rather than throw in the towel in the face of complexity (as many companies do, by not even *attempting* to track savings to the P&L), the more sophisticated PE firms work tirelessly to incrementally improve their savings conversion rate ... in the full knowledge that they will likely never get to 100%. "Every dollar saved is $10 in valuation ... "

What Can Non-PE Learn from PE?

As a Procurement consultant, I can tell you that having the PE parent actively involved is incredibly helpful ... they buy into the target, they invest for it, they push during execution, and they are a higher authority that can exert pressure when you need help. PE is a huge ally to any Procurement consultant and should be a huge ally to any ambitious CPO. It seems to me that owner involvement can be a very good thing. So much for separation of ownership and management, or maybe that's more appropriate for the large multi-nationals. Certainly, at the countless mid-cap companies ($400m to $2b in revenues) we've seen, the extra push and focus that PE can bring goes a long way and represents a huge opportunity for Procurement.

So, what can we learn from this? If Procurement is successful in a PE environment, it's because there is a strong sponsor who gets it and who is willing to invest for results; there is a highly incentivized owner who pushes hard to overcome the obstacles that lie in the path of Procurement teams; there is a non-acceptance of the status quo or sacred cows, and there is someone with the power and ability to lubricate the cross-functional interaction.

Other companies can't replicate the PE ownership environment, but we can learn from it. When I look at Private Equity and Procurement, I see PE doing two things: (i) sponsoring the Procurement function to make a splash, and then, (ii) helping in the journey by pushing it through cross-functionally. And that's really all there is to it, at the end of the day. Procurement needs to be given the right remit and platform, and then it needs the help of the rest of the C-Suite to help remove roadblocks and push it through.

In the end, the lessons your authors have learned from Procurement in action within the PE environment, are the same lessons as the overall lessons learned from this book. PE is just a good example of those lessons being put into practice:

- Give Procurement the remit and the resources it needs to succeed.
- Set an ambitious target and get alignment to this across functions and business lines.
- Structure the effort into a high visibility, CEO-sponsored program.
- Address large chunks of spend on a total cost basis.
- Push the sourcing teams forward relentlessly, removing obstacles in their path.
- Keep an eagle eye on the development of savings, from Target to Realized.
- Transition from the Program Environment to Business as Usual and continue to deliver year-on-year.

At the end of the day, Private Equity shows us that a Procurement transformation can be achieved relatively quickly and starting from a very low base (mid-cap companies with limited Procurement functions). It also shows us that executive level interest in, sponsorship of, and investment in the Procurement function make all the difference. And that's ultimately the lesson to be learned.

As well as working with PE, we the authors also have significant experience working in larger, publicly traded companies.

These companies almost invariably have bigger, more professional Procurement functions than their PE brethren. But the profit incentive can be diluted in these larger organizations, and the support and push that Procurement so desperately needs can be more difficult to mobilize. The experience of PE shows us that these soft success factors are in fact the most critical ... and, if we get them right, then we're off to a very good start.

Of course, following the example of PE is not the complete answer. But it'll get you out of the starting blocks with the odds stacked in your favor. And that's an appropriate analogy—PE is great at getting Procurement into and out of the starting blocks. But the sprinting is still down to the CPO and the rest of the C-Suite.

13

ROADMAP: Making a Concrete and Realistic Plan

This chapter assumes that you are a CPO, CFO, or CEO; that you're looking to make a major profit impact through Procurement; that Procurement is currently not optimized; and that a program of change will be required to make improvements to the function and to generate the savings. You're looking to maximize Procurement's impact—so where do you start? How do you get from today to a place where Procurement has been optimized and is delivering significant benefits to the business year-on-year?

Well, as with everything worth having, there's a journey involved. A gradual transformation. Ideally, in fact, an 18-month (or thereabouts) Procurement Transformation Program. Without such a program, you just won't receive the same level of attention, focus, and resource.

It's difficult to make a splash by just carrying on—particularly if there's a history of Procurement not having the right remit towards the business. Yes, the authors of this book are consultants, who are naturally biased towards a "program." But over the last 25 years, we've learned that there is a very strong correlation between success and the degree to which there is a formal, high visibility program of work.

This program needs to make a splash, so it needs to be high impact, high visibility, cross-functional, and fully resourced, so that it delivers significant savings for the business: An 18-month program, by the end of which you will have built an excellent Procurement function, and you will have delivered very sizeable savings to the business.

A well-designed Procurement transformation program has two fundamental and linked objectives: (i) to build a strong, cross-functionally integrated Procurement function, while (ii) using that function to deliver significant savings and other Procurement benefits to the business.

You can, of course, do this sequentially, first building your function, and then using this improved function to deliver the savings. Perfectly logical, right? Problem is, (i) you will lose a year: while you build your team, you will cost the business money and deliver nothing incremental, and (ii) you will miss out on what we call the "learning and transforming by doing" principle.

Transforming by Doing

At the core of your transformation is Strategic Sourcing, or category management. At the end of the day, you're looking to upskill your Procurement team so that they use a sophisticated Strategic Sourcing process to deliver benefits to the business. And again, you could spend six months giving your buyers classroom training in Strategic Sourcing before letting them loose on the business. Well, we all know that classroom training can only achieve so much; infinitely better if your people learn the new process *on the job*. That way, you get the job done more quickly, and your people truly learn the new way of operating.

In my consulting career, pretty much every Procurement transformation I've helped clients effect has involved those dual objectives of improving the function while delivering breakthrough benefits to the business. Unfortunately, there is sometimes a temptation during these programs to go for the quick bucks while the functional transformation gets neglected.

Often this is done using consultants to do the leg work … which is absolutely fine, as long as the functional improvement work gets done so that when the consultants leave, your team is ready to take up the reins. In fact, it makes sense to use consultants during the early waves of Strategic Sourcing, (i) to act as interims while you build up your team, and (ii) to show your people the way. Chapter 11: Consultants, looked at how best to deploy consultants and how to wean yourself off their support and become self-sufficient as the transformation progresses.

The importance of "transforming by doing" or "delivering while learning" cannot be overestimated. The activities that your Procurement people perform, if they're performed well, naturally throw off savings as a by-product. And those savings are very interesting to the business—whereas, if you set out a plan to "transform only," by investing in new resources, training programs, and tools, but without *delivering* anything at the same time, then this is essentially just a cost and is unlikely to generate any excitement within the executive team.

Putting the Plan Together

Such a program is, of course, no small undertaking. It will need to be sanctioned and sponsored—ideally at CEO level—and so will require an extensive business case, including savings targets, investments to upgrade the function, and detailed work plans, as well as a cross-functional governance structure.

Your authors have helped countless CPOs and CFOs to develop and gain agreement to their Procurement transformation plans. In this chapter, our intent is to share our experience, by detailing the various components that should make up your plan. Once this plan is fully assembled and sanctioned, you're ready to strap in and take off on your journey.

But before we dive into the various elements of the plan, a few words about the importance of spending time with and *listening* to your stakeholders before you put your plan together.

Start by Talking to People ... or Even Listening to People!

If you're a new executive assuming the reins of the Procurement function, orient yourself by talking to as many stakeholders as you can:

- The CEO: What are his or her key priorities, and how can Procurement support them? Would they sponsor a Procurement transformation program and all that it involves in return for significant value generation?
- The CFO: You're a major weapon in the CFO's cost-reduction arsenal; how does he or she like to work, and how should you best work together?
- The Functional Heads: Where can you help them to manage their cost base? What do they expect from Procurement? Do they have any concerns about you sourcing their categories?
- The Business Unit Heads: Where do they see the value of Procurement? If large chunks of their spends are business unit-specific, then how can you help there?
- The Suppliers (often forgotten): How is it doing business with our organization? What improvement opportunities do they see? How could they help us to reduce costs? How can we help them in return?

In Procurement, as in many areas of life, you hear many diametrically opposing views: "the problem is that central Procurement does terrible group deals" versus "the problem is that the local fiefdoms just don't comply." Your job is to assimilate and process these various opinions to probably arrive at a conclusion that sits somewhere in the middle. But you need to listen to your stakeholders—their expectations, needs, and requirements must be at the heart of your plan. You can't listen enough.

Armed with the insights from these conversations, you can set about the creation of your plan. So, let's take a quick look at the five key elements of the plan, as shown in **Figure 13.1.**

1) Procurement ambition and role

In Chapter 2, we looked in detail at the topic of "ambition." At the top of the pyramid that comprises your plan, needs to be some

Procurement Transformation Plan

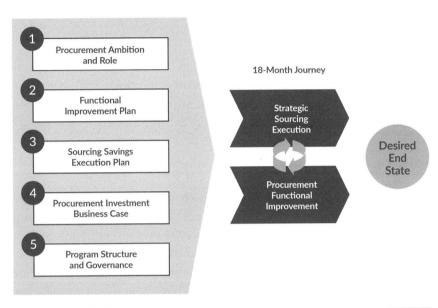

Figure 13.1 Procurement Transformation Plan

kind of vision and ambition for Procurement. In a way, the role or strategy for Procurement is predefined (to buy things that the business needs!)—the question is, how far do you want to stretch it? What do you want your Procurement function to be famous for? Can you articulate what is the next level for Procurement in your organization?

Your Procurement vision also needs to relate back to your corporate strategy. If your strategy is to grow aggressively by acquisition, an appropriate approach for Procurement is to (i) set itself up to be scalable, to keep adding new scope, and (ii) to set up an expert unit that takes the lead on integrating new acquisitions' spends. Or, if your corporate strategy is to digitize the business, Procurement can play a key part in this by digitizing the supply chain.

Next up is the role / remit / mandate. You're probably looking to strengthen these, so let's articulate what that looks like—maybe "working collaboratively with the business to jointly optimize its third party spend on a total cost basis." Another angle to take is to ask, how do you see Procurement's ways of working changing? How do you see your Procurement people interfacing with the rest of the business? Finally, think about the supplier side of the equation—what do you want your suppliers to say about you?

So, the first step is to really articulate where you want to get to. Chapter 2: Ambition, provides some useful examples of companies setting out different levels of Procurement ambition, based on their starting point and based on their level of aspiration.

2) Functional improvement plan

Next up is the detailed plan of how you're going to lick your Procurement function into shape. Here again, it's good to spend time listening to your internal customers to understand how Procurement is perceived today. Then you need to look at the various facets of the function—the organization, the people, the processes—and draw a line in the sand that says, "here's where we stand today." That's your starting point, and it needs to be realistic and ideally agreed to by Procurement and by the wider organization.

From that baseline, you can then develop a roadmap for your Procurement function. How good do you want to get, and in what timeframe? We find it useful to set a couple of objectives along the way—one after 12 to 18 months, and then another at three years in. That way, you break your ambition into a couple of chunks, and check your progress along the way.

The consultancies all have their "House of Procurement" or equivalent framework, and it's a useful one. It looks at the Procurement function in terms of its strategy, organization, people, processes, and systems, and it gives you a benchmark of what "bad," "average," and "good" look like. The following chart shows a version of such a tool **(see Figure 13.2)**.

Behind what you see in the summary depicted in Figure 13.2 are some 50 or so sub-factors and the relevant descriptors of a "1," "3," and "5" positioning. You need to eat the elephant in chunks, and set concrete objectives at the sub-factor level. For example, within "Procurement IT and Data," which systems are you going to implement and in

Functional Improvement Vision

Procurement Effectiveness—Current State and Future Vision

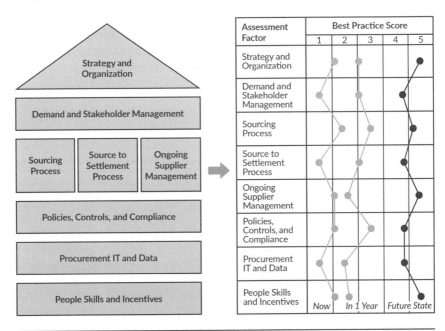

Figure 13.2   Functional Improvement Vision

what timeframe? Within "Policies, Controls, and Compliance," which policies are you going to draft and roll out by when?

These "House of Procurement" tools have their limitations, but I've seen them used extremely well by clients. At one large utility company, the entire Procurement team took part in a quarterly scoring across the 50 dimensions and, while doing so, discussed improvement opportunities and set new goals for the coming period. It was very powerful, and the framework became known as "the Worms Chart" (because the three lines look like wriggly worms!). If nothing else, it's a useful way of articulating a vision for the function, along with a concrete plan of what needs to be done to get there.

Ultimately, you need to take a long honest look at where you are today and determine where you want to be by when. The next chart illustrates the Procurement journey over time: plot your current state and ambition so you don't forget where you're headed (see Figure 13.3). And you don't need to reach for "World Class," certainly not in the medium-term. And, frankly, a professional services company doesn't need to have the same level of Procurement sophistication and centrality in the business as an auto manufacturer! Aim for "Advanced" instead; a good level of competence is all that's required.

In looking at the function and the team, we would also encourage the CPO to think about *activities*. Which activities *matter*… what are people doing, and how can we rebalance the mix? Often in Procurement, entire teams are doing entirely the wrong things, in which case you need a fundamental redesign rather than some

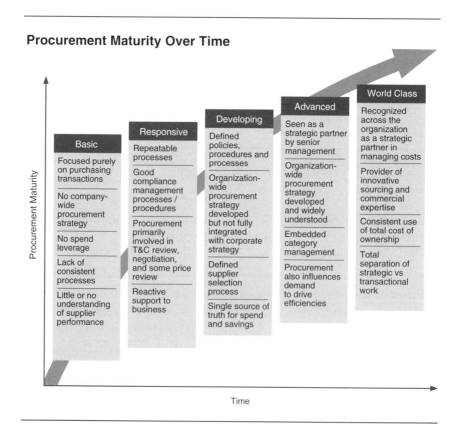

Figure 13.3 Procurement Maturity over Time

tweaking at the edges. And, if your team will be doing more meaningful activities in the future, you will likely need to upgrade the capability of the team.

In particular, you may need to invest in strategic Procurement resources, i.e., people who can do sourcing and category management. You may also need to re-organize the entire team to maximize their effectiveness on a global basis, balancing global coordination with local effectiveness (see Chapter 5: Operating Model).

Remember that the functional improvement plan needs to be granular and actionable. It's all very well saying, "We want to be at level X in Procurement maturity in 18 months"…but how are you going to get there? So, make sure you eat the elephant in chunks: What are you going to do, specifically, in the next six months, and then in the following six months? How are you going to know when you've been successful, not just at the end, but along key points in the journey?

Assembling the functional improvement plan is no easy task: you need to accept where you stand today, set a goal for the future, and develop a detailed plan for getting from the former to the latter. A central component of moving the function to the next level is to actually have your team execute a true Strategic Sourcing process across your spend…which brings us to the third element of the plan.

3) *Sourcing savings execution plan*

When the new CPO goes to the Board for approval of his or her Procurement plan, they are essentially pitching a business proposition, "Give me $10 million, and I'll bring you $50m in savings." So, you need to come up with a savings plan. What should this be based on?

There are many ways you could attack your third party spend to generate savings: you could do it supplier-by-supplier (although then you have no competition in play, it's just mano-a-mano); or you could do it by business unit (but then you miss out on any scale opportunity or spend leverage).

Clearly, the way to do it is by *category*: "Let's put all our laptop and desktop spend together and take it out to market." Makes sense. Most organizations have some 40–50 spend categories, so you now have 40 or 50 categories to play with. A category takes an average of six months to source—sounds long, but this includes harmonizing the spec up front, etc. So, classic sourcing theory says divide your spend into three waves of sourcing, making an 18-month program to work your way through the entire spend. Eighteen months also makes sense in reality, as unleashing more than a certain number of category-sourcing efforts becomes unmanageable for the wider organization.

Ultimately, and I oversimplify, the way you build such a plan is to set up a spreadsheet with the first two columns being "Category Name and Annual Spend," and the following columns being "% Addressed" and "Savings Low High %."

Now, estimate the addressability (it's normally no higher than 75%, because you can't get your arms around the tail spend of small suppliers and small countries, plus some spend is locked in); then estimate the savings potential. Aim for 8–10% and calibrate up or down … 3% for a commodity chemical, 12% for office supplies.

Next, sort in order of size and attractiveness and divide into three waves. Ta-dah! One sourcing savings plan … done! The beauty of it is the natural portfolio effect. Because you're attacking so many different categories with different budget-holders and different suppliers, you have a lot of balls in the air, and this spreads your risk. A couple of your categories might fall over; but another couple will hit the ball out the park and generate a 25% saving. The ability to spread your risk across categories is an important benefit of Strategic Sourcing.

What are the biggest pitfalls and reasons why people don't hit their proclaimed targets? Answer: addressability. Not only will you never include the various one-off purchases in your tail spend in your project but spend will "disappear" on you as you progress down the sourcing process.

That big outsourcing contract with IBM is for 10 years and can't really be touched; business unit X has pulled out of the effort; it turns out about 20% of the purchases in your category are bought for customers on a pass-through basis, thus lowering your savings. And so on, and so forth. SSS, we call it: Shrinking Spend Syndrome. It'll creep up on you, until your $100m scope has become $63m. You're still saving the projected 5–10% … but on a hopelessly smaller base. Plan for this phenomenon upfront by discounting each category by at least 25% for addressability—best advice you were ever given; trust us.

The by now (in)famous consulting bubble chart can actually be a useful tool **(see Figure 13.4)**. The example shown in this next chart was used with the newly minted CPO of a mobile telecoms operator. He wanted to drive a sourcing savings program across his four country units, each of which had its own powerful CPO. The country CPOs didn't want to play ball. The bubble chart was used to at least agree "*a*

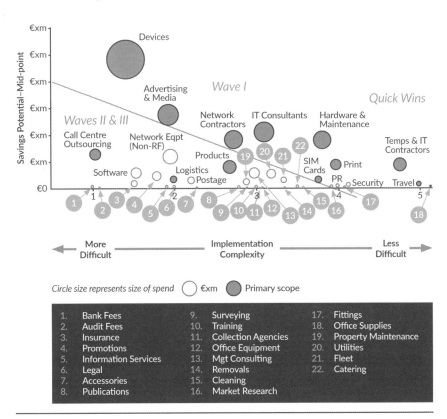

Figure 13.4   The Category Prioritization ("Bubble") Chart

handful of things where we could work together." Sitting in a conference room in Düsseldorf looking at a chart showing some 40 categories, it was only a matter of time before the group came up with *something* ... and that something turned into the first group-driven sourcing wave, which laid the groundwork for transforming the client's Procurement function. All down to the power of the humble sourcing bubble chart!

Without going into too much detail, the "bubble chart" plots categories based on savings potential and difficulty of implementation: How big is the prize? And how difficult is it to get? This makes a lot of sense in terms of prioritizing categories for sourcing. But it does require a lot of thought.

The savings potential of a category should be based on a number of factors: the addressable spend, your current state of Procurement sophistication in the category, the competitiveness of the supply market, and the existence of concrete, evidenced supply and demand-side improvement opportunities.

The other axis, implementation complexity, is also driven by a number of factors: Are there credible supplier alternatives? How difficult / costly is it to switch suppliers? And, just as importantly, what is the internal complexity: how on-board are the stakeholders, how difficult will it be to streamline specifications, can we actually push this through? In 80% of cases, the supply-side difficulties can be overcome relatively easily as long as you're not faced with a monopolistic supplier, which is relatively rare. So therefore, in practice, it's your assessment of the internal "do-ability" that matters more.

In terms of selecting the bubbles for that first wave—as the chart suggests, try to go for a mix of high savings and easy / quick-win opportunities. Try to have Wave 1 represent close to 50% of your total addressed spend, to maximize impact. If your Procurement team has yet to earn its stripes, start with the indirects, and maybe throw in one or two directs as a test case. Don't go just for the easy stuff ... that's not a way to start a transformation! And try to cover the whole business in terms of stakeholders—Manufacturing, Engineering / product development, IT / technology, Real Estate, Marketing, HR ... again, to maximize the portfolio effect, and to make sure that Procurement starts to penetrate all areas.

What's key is that you select categories in which you have strong budget-holder buy-in. So, you will need to iterate your bubble chart based on business priorities and stakeholder appetite. Stakeholder buy-in and appetite are more predictive of success in sourcing a category than anything else.

One final thing to consider when building your sourcing execution plan, and that is timing. Non-Procurement people typically vastly underestimate the time and effort required to properly source a category. Gathering baseline demand data, working with the budget-holders to harmonize the specification or to de-proliferate the items bought, soliciting supplier bids, holding several rounds of negotiations... the process is extremely thorough, which is why it throws off breakthrough savings.

On average, it takes six months to strategically source a category: two months for developing the baseline and agreeing to the strategy, and four further months from issue of RFP to supplier selection. Some categories can be done more quickly (Office Supplies, Temp Labor, Laptops can take four months), and some take nine months or longer, particularly if supplier certification is required at the end of the process.

I've spent half my career defending why six months is needed on average! A big driver of the time taken is the stakeholder intensiveness of the process. Yes, it will take six months rather than three, but at the end of the six months, *everyone* will be *fully* on board. Rush it in three months, and it will likely wobble and fall over at the end. You must make sure you have six months to complete a wave of sourcing; the business will need to be patient, it'll be worth the wait—and it's six months, we're not talking two years!

You will get push-back with regards to your savings plan, so you'll have to fight your corner. You'll be told that the spend in question is "in contract," so cannot be touched ... this is usually a fallacy. In-contract sourcing is absolutely possible, and the incumbent supplier will usually comply with the process—unless they're a particularly powerful IT company. You will get defensiveness from the business, and you have to *push* them beyond their comfort zone; as a CPO, that's part of your job. If a transformation doesn't feel uncomfortable, then it's just BAU, and that's not a transformation.

Now ... enough about the savings you're promising to the business! Let's look at the other side of the financial equation; i.e., what kind of investment are you going to ask for?

4) Procurement investment business case

You've got your sourcing savings plan. You now need to estimate the level of investment required in the Procurement function in order to make those savings happen. The good news is, and assuming that your organization is of a reasonable size, the ROI from Procurement is usually very attractive.

In your business case, there are four types of cost you will want to think about:

- The cost of hiring additional strategic Procurement resources.
- The costs associated with exiting any departing Procurement team members.
- The costs of new Procurement IT systems and tools.
- The cost of external consultancy support.

The people costs should be obvious—you're bringing in more, and more expensive, resources. The costs of IT will obviously depend on what systems you need to put in place. When it comes to IT, make sure you're comfortable with the business case: be aware that large cost over-runs are common, and that the financial benefits often ascribed to P2P are dependent on other workstreams—you will never realize the compliance savings associated with a P2P system if you haven't put any preferred suppliers in place.

What about consultancy support? One does see a lot of Procurement transformations heavily supported by consultants. That's because, as discussed earlier, consultants can fill in for your as-yet-incomplete Procurement team, enabling you to get going on savings delivery straightaway. In addition, the consultants will bring the required best practice processes and show your team how it's done.

You kick start the transformation with consultants doing a lot of the lifting, and over a period of 12–18 months, you gradually replace them with your new team members. Different organizations have different opinions on external consultants, and they do have to be used effectively (see Chapter 11: Consultants). However, there can be no doubt that the consultancies can stand up an instant team for you, which enables you to start generating benefits much sooner than you otherwise would.

The Procurement transformation business case then, involves (i) you pledging to deliver a specific savings target, for which (ii) the business sanctions your investment proposal. As long as your spend is of a reasonable magnitude, then the ROI on the exercise should be very attractive.

Ballpark, organizations tend to have very roughly one strategic Procurement person for each $20 million in spend (although this varies by industry). So, if you have $400m in spend, you might need a Procurement team of about 20 category management grade people. That might cost you around $1m per annum, versus a spend of $400m, out of which you could strategically source at least $200m, maybe $300m, and generate savings of $20m plus. These numbers are highly illustrative, but you get the point: $20m of savings from a $1m team is a fantastic ROI, even after you spend a few more million on Procurement technology and consultancy.

5) Program structure and governance

In Chapter 3: Sourcing Execution, we discussed how to set up a sourcing program for success. We talked about the need for full and active cross-functional engagement at all levels: within the sourcing teams, but also in the Steering Committee.

A Procurement transformation program is broader than a sourcing project. The program is typically divided into a number of workstreams: on the one side are the sourcing teams, executing the new Strategic Sourcing process; on the other side are the functional improvement workstreams: organization and operating model redesign; recruitment; sourcing, supplier management, and P2P process redesign; process roll-out and training; and IT systems partner selection and implementation. Assuming that the program progresses well, these two halves of the transformation give you the ammunition to tell an awesome story: "In the last six months, our sourcing teams delivered $5m in savings, while we filled a number of vacancies in the team and kicked off the implementation of System X." Nice.

Be very sure though, that the delivery workstreams and the transformation workstreams are intertwined. The sourcing teams should use the new Strategic Sourcing process to source their categories ... and get the buyers and the stakeholders used to the process. It's "learning while doing" at its best—the only way your people will adopt a new process is by learning it on the job.

One last word on program structure: I'm stating the obvious, but make sure that your sourcing teams are fully resourced. These teams should be *truly cross-functional* in nature. That does *not* mean that it's a Procurement-driven project, and the business doesn't have to provide any resources.

Our experience tells us that cross-functional teams just deliver more. In fact, the most successful sourcing programs I've seen have been *co-driven* by the business, to the extent that some of the sourcing teams were actually *led* by a person from the business, rather than by a Procurement person. And, to again state the obvious, the more of these people's time you can get, the better.

In an ideal world, the business would second its best resources to your program full time for six months. In reality, you may not get this—but don't settle for anything less than *formally seconded* team members, who have a significant proportion of their time, i.e., at least 15–20%, dedicated to the program.

Putting It All Together

To put together the previous five items will take a little time; in fact, it will take you three to four months. It's not quick, and it's not easy. But it's far better to launch your program when you've had proper time for planning and reflection first.

Your transformation plan needs to pull all five elements into an integrated 18-month program timeline, which might run something like this:

- Months 1 to 6: design organization, start recruitment, launch first set of sourcing teams with external consulting support.
- Months 6 to 12: your team is coming together now; source the next set of categories, with your people taking the lead, with reduced consulting support.
- Months 12 to 18: your team is now fully in place; conduct third wave of sourcing without any external support.
- Months 18 to 24: consolidate the function and shift to an ongoing category management cycle, re-sourcing each category every three years.

We have talked extensively about the need for executive sponsorship. So be sure that, in your plan, you ask not only for the financial investment that you require ... but you insist that the C-Suite invest their *time* into the effort.

Getting It Bought Off

Your plan is worth nothing of course, if there isn't alignment around it. And alignment is not enough—enthusiasm is what is required. Everyone in the same boat, going after those savings, a common goal. You really do need the CEO on board, as well as the CFO, COO, CIO, and the heads of the business / country units. So, socialize your plan extensively across this group, ask them to sign off on your plan, and ask all of them to be an active and engaged member of your Steering Committee.

Once your plan is signed off and any investment budget is secured, it's time to launch! Assemble the teams, ideally bring them together for a multi-day kick-off and planning session, and you're up and running.

Concluding Thoughts

As always in life, having a clear plan before you start is crucial, so don't go off half-cocked! Spend a few months figuring out your people, your internal stakeholders, and your suppliers. Your plan is really a Procurement business case—"Give me $X, and I will save you $Y." A great plan includes a clear, ambitious, credible, and realistic category savings plan, and a plan for building out the functional capability for the long run. So, don't cut corners—go structured, go deep, write it up properly.

Too many CPOs commit to savings targets without stating what they need from the company in return. Make your needs, as well as your commitments, explicit. And make sure that what you're launching is a high visibility, turbo-charged program—BAU is not going to deliver that 30% profit uplift.

Once your plan is approved, you need to be out the gates; so, the plan needs to be on the one hand visionary, but on the other very granular (Who are the 40–50 budget-holder team members starting on sourcing exercises tomorrow?). Ultimately though, as the saying goes, all plans fall apart upon contact, so what's more important is the underlying buy-in and visibility that your plan has. Once again, it's all about being cross-functionally aligned.

14

CONCLUSION: Summary and Final Thoughts

You've made it to the end of the book, and we really don't have much left to share at this point. Nothing to do but to recap the key messages that we'd like you to take away.

You will have noticed a number of themes that run across the chapters of this book. They are our key messages (**Figure 14.1**); if you remember nothing else, try to remember these. If tomorrow or next week or next year you design a Procurement transformation program for your organization, cross-reference your plan against these seven themes, and make sure you have all the right elements in place and are approaching them in the best possible way.

When you read these themes, you'll notice that none of them are rocket science, and none of them offer a huge "a-ha! moment." And that's because they are all straightforward, obvious things: good people, working cross-functionally, making sure the savings are credible. None of this is "next level Procurement," it's just strong Procurement that delivers results.

Chapters and Themes

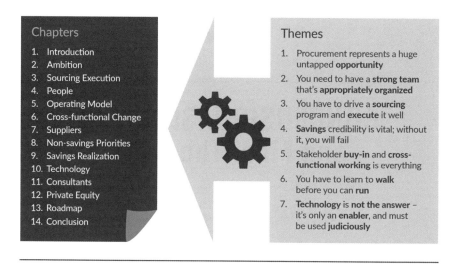

Chapters

1. Introduction
2. Ambition
3. Sourcing Execution
4. People
5. Operating Model
6. Cross-functional Change
7. Suppliers
8. Non-savings Priorities
9. Savings Realization
10. Technology
11. Consultants
12. Private Equity
13. Roadmap
14. Conclusion

Themes

1. Procurement represents a huge untapped **opportunity**
2. You need to have a **strong team** that's **appropriately organized**
3. You have to drive a **sourcing** program and **execute** it well
4. **Savings** credibility is vital; without it, you will fail
5. Stakeholder **buy-in** and **cross-functional working** is everything
6. You have to learn to **walk** before you can **run**
7. **Technology** is **not the answer** – it's only an **enabler**, and must be used **judiciously**

Figure 14.1   Chapters and Themes

Procurement Is Not Rocket Science, but It's Difficult to Do It Right

The fact is that most Procurement strategies, approaches, and ideas sound simple but can be very difficult to execute in practice. We think sourcing office supplies must be easy, because office supplies are not strategic to our organization. In reality, sourcing office supplies for a multi-national company is a very difficult feat, even when you have strong people and executive level backing. Whatever you do, it will only work if you execute well.

Good Procurement is all about good execution. Why? Because it's about playing middleman between one of your corporate functions and a set of external suppliers that want their business. You have to essentially use data and your intellect to broker a deal that works for both your organization and the winning supplier(s). That's a tough thing to do. All companies try to do the same things, all Travel category managers have a similar strategy ... but some execute it much better than others, and that's where the difference lies. And strong execution is, again: about good people, about working well within the organization, and about getting stuff done.

And of course, as always, there is no silver bullet or easy answer. It's hard, and it requires a strong commercial focus, ambition, relationship management skill, and the ability to persuade and take others with you. But, if you apply those skills you can unlock the value that resides in Procurement.

Let's quickly recap the seven themes and distil the key messages from the book to try to help you remember as much as possible once you put the book down.

1) Procurement represents a huge untapped opportunity

Well, I think we've made that much clear in this book. We've talked about how Procurement represents 50–80% of all costs depending on your industry, how maybe 60–70% is addressable in the medium-term, and how you can probably take out 10% in cost in aggregate, even if you already have a good Procurement team in place. We also talked about the fact that, for a typical manufacturing company with a 10% margin, these savings would yield a 36% uplift in EBITDA, a magnitude of opportunity that would be extremely difficult to find elsewhere.

Why is the opportunity untapped? We talked about the fact that relatively few organizations have reached Procurement best practice as exemplified by the automotive OEMs since the 1980s. How it's difficult to bring together all the elements required for success. How Procurement is on the one hand simple, but on the other hand difficult to execute. How Procurement came from an administrative, contracting place and doesn't enjoy the remit to challenge the business as an equal partner, which prevents it from reaching full potential savings. And how, in some cases, Procurement falsely believes itself to have already reached best practice ... or at least wants to convince others that it has done so ... which then results in the door to further value creation being firmly locked shut.

Finally, we started to introduce the theme of cross-functionality and the fact that sitting in a functional silo and casting itself as a group of professionals or, worse, a corporate policeman, is not a basis for unleashing the potential of Procurement.

2) You need to have a strong team that's appropriately organized

In anything you do, you need to have good people. Nowhere is this more true than in Procurement, where, to really optimize your spend, using all Procurement levers, you need people who are intelligent, numerate, commercial, analytical, motivated, persuasive, and impressive. That's because you need them to execute a very complicated task, namely sourcing (or facilitating the sourcing of) other people's requirements, often across geographies and markets.

If you're a CPO, your team's skill and competence is probably the most important thing in your transformation journey, and one that many companies don't get right.

We talked about how Procurement as a function often suffers from a skills deficit. And about how those skills are not about negotiation expertise, knowing sourcing processes, or knowing supply markets, but rather a mix of analytical / commercial and influencing skills. The latter are critical in a function that interfaces with, and has to influence, so many varied stakeholders across the organization.

These skills are also linked to the personal culture of your people—given the nature of the Procurement function, they need to see themselves as facilitators to the business, rather than as controllers. Good, strategic Procurement people also need a level of drive and motivation; they have to question why things are the way they are and push to change them. Finally, they need project management skills, since a Procurement function is ultimately a project function that sends resources out to complete projects for its internal clients.

We talked about the need to segregate strategic from non-strategic Procurement activities and people, and we discussed how training needs to be much broader than Procurement hard skills (such as negotiation, supply market analysis, and contracting), and focus heavily on soft skills (stakeholder management, influencing, presenting).

You can't grow or retain strong people if you don't have good career development, and we gave the example of the automotive OEMs that rotate their people across functions, leading to a much higher level of mutual respect and understanding between Procurement and Finance, Manufacturing, and Engineering. They feel part of the same team and work together relatively seamlessly. In order to succeed, Procurement must break out of its silo, and this also applies to its approach to career management.

We talked about the fact that, to build an optimum talent pool, Procurement should not hire exclusively from amongst Procurement veterans, but look to mix this up with people with non-Procurement backgrounds, for example, drawing in people from Finance, graduate trainees, and MBAs. This enriches the talent pool within Procurement, while promoting cross-functional working and integration.

Finally, Chapter 5: Operating Model, explored the need to *organize* your Procurement resources in the most impactful way—seeking to balance two things: (i) local internal client needs with the desire to aggregate spend centrally, and (ii) the need for category specialism with flexibility of deployment. No point recruiting even the strongest individuals if their position on the organigram hampers their effectiveness.

3) *You have to drive a sourcing program and execute it well*

A machine needs to have an engine room and, in the case of Procurement, that's Strategic Sourcing. Sourcing is the key deliverable from strategic Procurement, it's where Procurement pulls together the requirements, fulfils them, and in the meantime generates EBITDA value. Strategic Sourcing should make up most of the work of the strategic Procurement team, and it should deliver the lion's share of Procurement's savings.

We talked about how, when it comes to Strategic Sourcing, everybody does it, but few do it well. That it has roots in 1980s "Big Auto," and is really nothing more than a logical, structured, holistic way to take out large swaths of external cost. What sets it apart is good execution on the one hand, and proper cross-functional collaboration on the other.

A properly executed multi-wave Strategic Sourcing program allows the CPO to attack the *annualized* spend in each category, rather than just sourcing each contract as it falls due. To do it properly is to address all savings levers including, crucially, the specifications. Combining fundamental spec revision with well-executed supply market leverage is what gets results.

We talked about seven step methodologies—about how they're all the same, but the difference is the degree to which they are being *applied*—and applied in an effective manner. "Box-tick sourcing" is the enemy of Procurement value creation, and we discussed how to avoid it.

Tied to the theme of Strategic Sourcing is the theme of good execution. Strategic Sourcing is not rocket science, and in fact the seven steps seem remarkably simple and straightforward. The magic lies in how well they're executed, and that in turn is down to execution excellence at the working level—the baseline, the supply market analysis, the supplier list, the tender documentation, the sourcing strategy, the cross-functional engagement. If these things are done well, then savings and credibility will follow.

Sourcing underlies everything we do in Procurement. It's how we add value, it's how we make savings, it's how we're viewed by the rest of the business. It needs to be structured, holistic, data-driven, project-managed, cross-functional, empowered, and high quality. Then the CPO will shine, the savings will be co-owned, the sourcing solutions will be good for the end customer ... and your chosen suppliers will be happy! Do sourcing badly on the other hand, and you're a laughingstock internally and not trusted by suppliers.

Linked to the need for good sourcing is of course ... the credibility of your savings.

4) *Savings credibility is vital; without it, you will fail*

The importance of savings to Procurement cannot be understated, hence the dedication of an entire chapter of this book to the subject. If sourcing is the engine room of Procurement, then savings are the lifeblood.

We talked about how, first, the savings actually need to be operationally delivered, and they need to be significant—well beyond BAU savings, such as cost-avoidance and short-term discounts. They need to encompass the total spend and take a total cost perspective. The best mechanism for driving these types of savings is a sourcing program, because it addresses annual spend across the company and because it allows the savings to be real and evident.

Then the savings need to be defined, measured, and tracked, and this is an area where most organizations fall short. The CPO should leverage the Finance function for this and needs to make the CFO his or her best friend and ally. Finance needs to be very closely involved at every step of the sourcing process—from baseline validation through to budget cut—and it needs to understand every number along the way. Finance involvement also helps drive consistent numbers over time, thereby avoiding surprises at the end. We suggested tracking savings over time through the stages of Target, Identified, Negotiated, Contracted, Signed-off, Implemented, Budgeted, and Realized.

We discussed at length the many "leakage points" that exist along a saving's "journey" to the P&L; about the need for proper follow-up, if savings are to be realized and sustained. We described the classic problem whereby the ongoing management of the category (and of its suppliers) falls between two stools when Procurement pulls out post-sourcing process. How it's no surprise then when it turns out there is only 27% compliance with our fancy new sourcing deal. How companies don't actually measure compliance with deals and policies, but that they need to, and that the compliance mechanism needs to have actual teeth in order to be successful.

Finally, we looked at the topic of budgeting, aka "if you don't take the money away, there won't be a saving." Again, our advice is to work very closely with Finance so that they can validate and vouch for the numbers at each step. We discussed the timing of "taking the money away," with it ideally coming in as a haircut *before* Procurement is set loose, rather than after the fact, so as to position the function as a helper to the budget-holder.

5) *Stakeholder buy-in and cross-functional working is everything*

We talked about the fact that there are two key internal stakeholder sets for Procurement, (i) the budget-holder (it's their money!), and

(ii) Finance (they need to be able to bank any savings at the end). Buy-in from these stakeholders needs to come bottom-up based on category-by-category delivery and credible numbers—real savings.

To gain buy-in to a category-level sourcing decision, the budget-holder needs to feel that his or her needs have been listened to, that he or she has been fully involved, to feel very comfortable with the supplier selection decision (to fully own that decision, in fact) ... so buy-in is the product of spending *time* with that person.

Buy-in is also based on being persuasive, and much persuasion is in turn based on having credible facts and figures. The degree of buy-in is always at least *partly* down to the quality of one's materials—the baseline, the RFP document, the savings business case. If these work products are impressive, buy-in is that much easier to attain.

You may say that stakeholder buy-in and cross-functional working are two sides of the same coin, and you'd be right! You certainly cannot get any buy-in unless you're working cross-functionally in an effective manner. And cross-functional is not just a buzzword; neither is it an *option* ... it's what actually needs to happen for Procurement to be successful. And it's, again, that triumvirate of Procurement, Finance, and the budget-holder function. If between them they are aligned, and they say, "We will from now on buy 80% of XYZ from Suppliers A, B, and C only, and that results in a cost reduction of $X", then it's a done deal, the savings will follow.

Cross-functional working is not just a buzzword. Rather, again it's the triumvirate of purse string holder, budget-holder, and commercial influencer. And what does cross-functional working mean anyway? It just means working collaboratively and involving all parties fully, rather than operating out of a silo, telling people what to do, and making decisions without full consultation.

And in the context of Strategic Sourcing, working cross-functionally means having *full* cross-functional involvement at all levels of the project org chart. That means that some of the sourcing teams should ideally be *led* by individuals from other functions, and it means that the CEO, CFO, and CIO actually need to show up for the Steering Committee meeting, otherwise it will fail.

Which brings us neatly to our final point, which is about executive sponsorship. This is required to permit the *possibility* that Procurement can work with the other functions. And it's all too often lacking. How high up the chain does it need to go? The answer is the C-Suite, and more specifically the CFO, who is an absolutely critical part of the success recipe. He or she mustn't be the enemy of Procurement, asking, "Where the hell are those savings you promised me?" at the end of the year. They must be the CPO's best friend—helping to build the baseline, to sign off on the savings, and to ultimately remove them from budgets.

Above all else, in working cross-functionally and in garnering buy-in, Procurement must remember its position, which is to serve the budget-holder. It's their money not Procurement's, so it needs to act like it—respectfully, courteously, professionally.

6) *You have to learn to walk before you can run*

Simple, really. But you'd be surprised. Just don't set the bar too high, that's all we're saying. Let's not get over-excited. And setting the bar at the right height has two components. Component 1 is recognizing where the bar is today, which may be lower than you assume, and Component 2 is setting the aspiration (in terms of the size, breadth, and timing of your ambition) at an appropriate level.

In Chapter 8: Non-savings Priorities, we talked about the non-savings related Procurement goals, which are often seen as "higher order" goals. I've had countless CPOs tell me that "we're moving away from savings as our primary measure;" even that "we're now seen as a profit center rather than just a cost center." Ambition is good, but let's learn to walk before we run.

As we discussed in Chapter 2: Ambition, too many Procurement functions set their ambitions at too lofty a level. The reality is that, when a Procurement function is truly excellent, it is then recognized as such, and its role will then naturally be expanded or enlarged. Get the basics right, and the rest will follow.

The same caution applies to the timing of your ambitions. Many CPOs set out to achieve too much too quickly. Or are pushed to achieve more quickly, often in the shape of in-year savings or quick wins. Extreme care needs to be taken here. Proper Procurement takes time … in particular, the time to care for, nurture, and win over stakeholders. Cut that time short, and the exercise reverts to being transactional, with minimal chance of true alignment. If it could be done quickly and easily, why wasn't it done before? Exactly. Because it's difficult, a lot of people need to agree, and it takes time. So, particularly in the early months of a Procurement transformation, let's take it one step at a time, one dollar saved at a time. Rome wasn't built in a day.

One last thought regarding walking and running. Too many Procurement leaders spend far too much time complaining about "the business not allowing us to play." Again, it's a case of wanting to run before you can walk. Until you've proven yourself, the business is not going to throw open the door and roll out a red carpet for you. You have to earn their trust, you have to earn that mandate … if you deliver, believe me, that door will be opened.

7) Technology is not the answer—it's only an enabler, and must be used judiciously

In Chapter 10: Technology, we talked about Procurement systems, and that the pace of technological development is accelerating exponentially. On the one hand, Procurement needs to embrace new technological developments—Procurement is the facilitator of the buying process, and it needs to ultimately strive to make that process slicker, easier, and more user-friendly. After all, Procurement's customers are accustomed to using Amazon-like user interfaces in their private lives and will hold these up as their benchmark.

At the same time, we cautioned against "rushing out" to buy the latest technology tools in the mistaken belief that technology is the answer. It's not, it's merely an enabler, and one that can only fulfil its function if (i) the processes it supports are fit-for-purpose, and (ii) the users of these tools actually adopt them. When it comes to tools such as Spend Analytics, Contract Management, and E-sourcing, we've seen countless examples of companies buying entire suites of these products, only to completely fail to drive their adoption; in fact, in our experience this is a very common phenomenon.

Why? Because everything *around* the tool is not ready: the data is not available, the intended users are not trained in the tool's use, or the processes that the tool hopes to automate are designed without the tool in mind. The implication is clear—too many companies put the cart before the horse. Instead of starting with the software tool and its promised benefits, let's start by focusing and fixing the inputs to these tools. That means harvesting, cleaning, and owning your data and then fitting the tool around it, rather than vice versa. A contract management tool won't automatically optimize your disparate (and often non-existing / poor quality) contracts … you need to create and / or collect them first! Sounds ridiculously obvious, but we've seen too many examples of empty contract management tools! Avoid the steam-powered Tesla!

Technology disruption is a reality, and Procurement teams need to have a digitalization roadmap or run the risk of becoming an irrelevance in their organizations because users opt out of difficult-to-use Procurement processes.

But IT systems can only ever be part of the answer. You can't spend your way to success by buying Procurement systems and then not using them properly. So, do your homework, choose the right functionality and provider, be realistic about your expectations on costs, savings, and timing … but most importantly, make sure that your Procurement team is ready for these systems. If they don't know how to run a Strategic Sourcing process, then a fancy e-sourcing system is not going to help.

Breaking Down Silos

These are the key themes of this book. And the primary "theme of themes," running across all these themes, is the fact that Procurement is a cross-functional endeavor. Procurement cannot be done effectively by the CPO alone, sitting in a functional silo. And conversely, it doesn't pay for the rest of the C-Suite to sit back and "look to Procurement to deliver it, that's their job." Wrong! It's *not* their job! It's your money, so why would it be their job to look after it?

The fact is that it's a *company-wide* endeavor. It's the triumvirate of Procurement, Finance, and budget-holder functions, working together to generate outcomes that work for all parties. It's about Procurement busting out of its silo to effect a wave of value across the business—value that's extracted jointly, balancing the needs of the users with the constraints around costs. And value that can be measured and found in the P&L account at the end of the year.

Well, that's about all, folks. We hope this book has opened your eyes about Procurement and what it can do and has left you with some good advice as you look to maximize the potential of Procurement in your organization.

We wish you the very best of luck as you embark on your exciting journey.

The End

Acknowledgments

We would like to thank a number of contributors from Efficio. Our thanks for their insights and help go to Ian Bolger, Declan Feeney, Toby Munyard, Pauline Potter, Rene Schalk, James Symonds, and Peter Wetherill.

We would like to say a special thank you to Tina Stone, Efficio's Marketing and Communications Strategist, for managing us through the writing process from beginning to end, and for making sure we hit our deadlines. And thank you to Marianne McAlindon for starting and seizing this opportunity.

A big thank you also to Mike Campbell at Wiley, for making our writing and publishing experience an enjoyable one.

And finally, we would like to thank our wives, Michelle, Sonja, and Inês, for putting up with our countless "writing weekends."

About the Authors

Alex Klein

ALEX KLEIN is the COO of Efficio, which he co-founded in 2000. Prior to this, he was a Principal with A.T. Kearney, for whom he worked for seven years in its London and New York offices. Alex is a leading expert in Procurement and helps companies to design and execute multi-national and global Procurement transformation programs.

Alex's experience spans the Automotive, Manufacturing, Utilities, Telecommunications, Technology, and Financial, and Professional Services industries. He also works extensively with the world's leading Private Equity firms to optimize the Procurement capabilities and costs of their portfolio companies.

Being a co-founder, Alex has helped to grow Efficio from a six-person start-up in 2000, into the world's largest specialist Procurement consultancy, with some 500 employees based in offices across Europe, North America, and the Middle East. He led the firm's market-facing activities in its early years, and established Efficio's first North American office in New York.

Alex holds an MBA from Manchester Business School and a BA with First-Class Honours from the University of Bristol. He is bilingual in German and English, and he speaks fluent French and Spanish. He is a keen classical guitarist and recently walked the 500-mile (790 km) Camino de Santiago.

Alex lives in Ascot, England, and Valencia, Spain, with his wife Michelle, his sons Max and Felix, and a chow chow called Juri.

Simon Whatson

SIMON WHATSON is a Vice President in Efficio's London office and joined the company in 2015. Since the start of his career, he has worked in a wide variety of Procurement consulting and industry roles at Wolseley, BrainNet Supply Management Consultants, and Oliver Wyman.

Simon is a senior program leader and supports organizations of all sizes to transform Procurement from a back office administrative support team to a core value function through multi-year programs. He works across all sectors but has significant experience in Utilities and Infrastructure, Financial Services, Pharmaceuticals, and Leisure & Tourism.

He is a recognized expert in digital Procurement and has chaired and spoken at global conferences on the topic. He has led Efficio's global thought leadership and market research studies in recent years that have focused on Procurement technology and talent. Simon has also been named a winner in *Supply & Demand Chain Executive's* 2021 Pros to Know award, which recognizes outstanding executives whose accomplishments offer a roadmap for other leaders looking to leverage supply chains for competitive advantage.

Simon holds a First-Class Honours degree in Mathematics from the University of Durham and, as well as his native English, speaks fluent French and German. He is a keen and dedicated triathlete and has recently represented Great Britain at the World Triathlon Championships at age group level. He lives in Newbury, England, with his wife Sonja and his three children Liam, Lucas, and Leon.

Jose Oliveira

JOSE OLIVEIRA is a Vice President in Efficio's New York office and joined the company in 2011. He has worked as a Procurement Consultant in four different continents with Efficio, A.T. Kearney, and Roland Berger.

He is predominantly focused on Procurement Transformation, primarily in the Services industry and with Private Equity clients.

He has worked in building up Procurement in several fast-growing, global market leaders in industries such as Software, Education, Retail, and Insurance.

Jose is the global practice lead for the Opportunity Assessment practice at Efficio and is particularly interested in helping Procurement departments establish themselves in areas with intense challenges around cross-functional collaboration.

He holds a Business Administration degree from the Portuguese Catholic University and speaks six languages fluently. He was a professional cellist with Sinfonietta de Lisboa and a competitive sailor. He has lived in seven different countries and currently is based in Orlando, Florida, with his wife Inês, his three children, Leonor, Lourenço, and Teresa, and a horse called Picasso.

List of Acronyms

AI	Artificial Intelligence
BAU	Business as Usual
B2B	Business-to-Business
B2C	Business-to-Consumer
Capex	Capital Expenditure
CEO	Chief Executive Officer
CFO	Chief Financial Officer
CIO	Chief Information Officer
CIPS	Chartered Institute of Procurement & Supply
COGS	Cost of Goods Sold
COO	Chief Operations Officer
CPO	Chief Procurement Officer
CSR	Corporate Social Responsibility
EBIT	Earnings Before Interest and Taxes
EBITDA	Earnings Before Interest, Taxes, Depreciation, and Amortization

ERP	Enterprise Resource Planning
Exco	Executive Committee
Fintech	Financial Technology
FM	Facilities Management
FMCG	Fast-moving Consumer Goods
FP&A	Financial Planning and Analysis
IT	Information Technology
JIT	Just-in-Time
KPIs	Key Performance Indicators
MECE	Mutually Exclusive and Collectively Exhaustive
MRO	Maintenance, Repair, and Operations
NLP	Neuro Linguistic Programming
Non-COGS	Non-Cost of Goods Sold
OEM	Original Equipment Manufacturer
Opex	Operating Expenses
Ops	Operations
P&L	Profit and Loss
PE	Private Equity
PMO	Project Management Office
P2P	Purchase to Pay
RFI	Request for Information
RFP	Request for Proposal
ROI	Return on Investment
SKUs	Stock-keeping Units
SSS	Shrinking Spend Syndrome
TCO	Total Cost Ownership
TINCSIBR	Target, Identified, Negotiated, Contracted, Signed-off, Implemented, Budgeted, and Realized
VCP	Value Creation Plan

Index

Page numbers in *italics* reference figures